EARLY YEARS AROUND THE YEAR

CW00741930

Physical development

Seasonal activities

Pauline Kenyon

Seasonal ideas ◆ Festival activities ◆ Early learning goals

CREDITS

British Library Cataloguing-in-Publication Data
A catalogue record for this book is available from the British Library.

ISBN 0 439 01909 5

AUTHOR
Pauline Kenyon

EDITOR
Sally Gray

ASSISTANT EDITOR
Saveria Mezzana

SERIES DESIGNER
Anna Oliwa

DESIGNER
Paul Roberts

ILLUSTRATIONS
Jenny Tulip

COVER ILLUSTRATION
Anna Hopkins

ACKNOWLEDGEMENTS
The publishers gratefully acknowledge permission to reproduce the following copyright material:

Qualifications and Curriculum Authority for the use of extracts from the QCA/DfEE document *Curriculum Guidance for the foundation stage* © 2000, Qualifications and Curriculum Authority.

Text © 2001 Pauline Kenyon
© 2001 Scholastic Ltd

Published by Scholastic Ltd, Villiers House, Clarendon Avenue, Leamington Spa, Warwickshire CV32 5PR

Designed using Adobe Pagemaker
Printed by Proost NV, Belgium

Visit our website at www.scholastic.co.uk

1 2 3 4 5 6 7 8 9 0   1 2 3 4 5 6 7 8 9 0

 CONTENTS

Around the year

The aims of this series
This book forms part of a series of six books covering the six areas of learning and provides activities to support the Early Learning Goals (QCA). They offer practitioners working with young children, in any type of setting, a wide range of activities to use throughout the year that are linked to seasonal and festival-based themes. Childminders and parents will also find the activities easy to organize and valuable.

The Early Learning Goals
The activities in this book focus on the requirements for the Early Learning Goals for Physical development which form part of the overall Foundation Stage curriculum, as determined by the Department for Education and Employment (DfEE) and Qualifications and Curriculum Authority (QCA). Each specific Early Learning Goal for Physical development is covered within the wide range of activities planned in this book, intended for use across the year.

The activities in this book are also closely linked and designed to reinforce the Early Learning Goals for all the other Areas of Learning within the curriculum – for example, many of the activities encourage development of the children's respect for their own and other cultures (Personal, social and emotional development).

The ideas suggested in this book can be applied equally well to the documents on pre-school education published for Scotland, Wales and Northern Ireland.

How to use this book
The book contains four chapters, one for each season. The first six activities in each section are linked to general seasonal themes. The other eight are linked to festivals and cultural events from many backgrounds, celebrated

during specific seasons of the year. They are presented in chronological order to make curriculum planning easier.

Every activity within each chapter has clear learning objectives and is laid out with easy-to-follow guidance. The resources required are kept simple and are generally limited to those that are readily available or easily obtainable in most settings for under-fives. Many of the activities are supported by photocopiable sheets which are designed to make busy practitioners' preparations easier and to capture the children's imaginations. Where an activity involves handling of food, this symbol (!) will remind you to check for any allergies and dietary requirements.

The activities are designed for groups of different sizes, from small groups to whole groups. Each activity provides a clear outline of how to introduce and develop different physical sessions. Many involve both fine motor co-ordination work and gross motor tasks and all are focused on play activities to effectively promote young children's learning. Many activities have been planned in such a way that they can be undertaken inside or outside, depending on the weather. Although some activities will be best served by using a large clear space, group sizes can be adjusted to suit the actual space available.

This book has been written to meet the needs of practitioners working in various settings and with children of different ages and abilities. The 'Support' section gives suggestions about how the main activity can be adapted for younger children or those with special needs, and the 'Extension' section explains how the main activity can be extended for older or more able children. There are also helpful suggestions at the end of each activity for how links with parents and carers can be strengthened, so that the children's physical development can be productively extended and reinforced at home and positive home/setting partnerships be forged.

Displays and performances

Many of the activities contained in this book will result in the children making exciting items, such as masks and instruments, that can contribute to colourful displays. These would usefully provide a whole setting focus on a multitude of cultural events and celebrations which will support the children's experience of multicultural education and the pluralist world in

which they live. Additionally, many of the activities can be easily developed into performances, presentations and assembly items that are ideal for sharing with parents and carers, other children and the community.

Curriculum planning using this series

This book links closely with the other books in this series, which cover the other Areas of Learning of Personal, social and emotional development; Communication, language and literacy; Mathematical development; Knowledge and understanding of the world and Creative development. Activities in all the series' books neatly dovetail together without replication and form a very useful overall resource for learning.

This book can be used as a central programme of themes to be followed, planned into an annual cycle or over a longer period. Where settings need to plan a two-year cycle to avoid repetition for children of different ages, particular activities can be selected to fit into a full 24-month programme. This book can also be dipped into, to choose individual activities which will support other scheduled work on the seasons or selected festivals and events.

Practitioners can be confident that the seasonal schedule contained in this book will enable them to cover a wide range of activities which address all the Early Learning Goals for Physical development in an imaginative and exciting way.

Festivals

Purim (March)
Jewish festival recalling how Queen Esther saved the Jews from being killed by the trickery of an evil man called Haman.

Mother's Day (March/April)
Once a holiday for servant girls to visit their mothers with gifts, it is now a time to show love and appreciation to mothers.

Easter (March/April)
The most important Christian festival when Jesus' return to life is celebrated. People give chocolate eggs as a symbol of new life.

April Fool's Day (1 April)
A day when people can play tricks on one another up to midday.

Baisakhi (14 April)
The Sikh New Year festival commemorating the five volunteers that offered to sacrifice themselves at Guru Gobind Singh's request. Also marks the introduction of the Khalsa.

St George's Day (23 April)
The patron saint of England is supposed to have slain an evil dragon who was devouring humans. He may be based on a Christian Roman soldier who spent his life fighting evil.

Kodomono-hi/Japanese Children's Day (5 May)
This happy festival has decorations focusing on strength and perseverance, symbolized by carp (for energy) and irises (like a Samurai's strong sword).

Wesak (May/June)
Theravada Buddhists celebrate the birth, enlightenment and death of the Buddha on this day. People decorate their temples and homes with candles, flowers and incense.

Shavuot (May/June)
A Jewish festival celebrating the revelation of the Ten Commandments to Moses on Mount Sinai. Synagogues are decorated with dairy foods, fruit and flowers during this festival.

Midsummer's Day (24 June)
Falls shortly after the longest day of the year. Druids still meet at Stonehenge for sunrise. Traditions include bonfires, feasts and torchlit processions.

Father's Day (June)
A special day to acknowledge the role of fathers and others who have similar caring roles. They are thanked with presents and cards.

Pentecost (June)
Seven weeks after Easter, Christians celebrate Pentecost, remembering how God sent flames which rested on the disciples' heads giving them the gift of being understood by people of all nationalities.

Dragon Boat Festival (June)
A Chinese festival honouring Ch'u Yuan who drowned himself in protest at the Emperor. Today dragon boat races symbolize the rush to save him.

O-bon (July/August)
The most important Buddhist festival in Japan – a time when families remember deceased relatives. They decorate their homes with flowers and lights and celebrate with feasting, dancing and tug-of-war contests.

Ganesh-chaturthi (August/September)
This Hindu festival celebrates the birth of Ganesh, the elephant-headed god. Ganesh is believed to help with new ventures such as moving house and marriages, and these events often take place during the festival.

Ethiopian New Year (11 September)
Celebrated by Rastafarians. Each year in the four-year-cycle is named after an evangelist. Celebrations include eating, drumming and dancing.

Chinese Moon Festival (September)
This Chinese festival remembers Chang Er, the wife of a wicked emperor who flew to the moon when her husband tried to kill her – she has lived there ever since. Moon cakes are eaten.

Sukkot (September/October)
A Jewish festival that commemorates the people's journey in the wilderness after escaping from Egypt. Temporary shelters decorated with fruit and vegetables are built and harvest is celebrated.

Harvest Festival (September/October)
A time of thanksgiving for the harvesting of crops. Traditions include harvest suppers and giving of food to the needy.

Navaratri (September/October)
Navaratri means nine nights. This is a Hindu festival where the people worship the goddess Durga, often performing stick dances and singing.

Divali (October/November)
Hindus remember the story of Rama and Sita. Sikhs celebrate the sixth Guru, Guru Hargobind's escape from imprisonment. Homes are decorated with divas (lamps).

Bonfire Night (5 November)
This British celebration commemorates Guy Fawkes' unsuccessful attempt to blow up the Houses of Parliament in 1605. Families celebrate with fireworks.

Hanukkah (November/December)
Jewish festival of light lasting eight days, commemorating the reclamation of the temple from the Syrians and the miracle of the temple light that burned for eight days on a small amount of oil.

Advent (December)
Christian period of preparation for Jesus' birth, beginning on the fourth Sunday before Christmas and ending on Christmas Day. Traditions include Advent candles and calendars.

Christmas Day (25 December)
Christian festival celebrating the birth of Jesus. People decorate their homes and exchange gifts as a reminder of those given to Jesus.

Eid-ul-Fitr (December/January)
Muslim festival held at the end of Ramadan. People wear new clothes, visit family and friends, exchange gifts and cards and eat a celebratory meal.

New Year (1 January)
New Year is celebrated with parties and the traditional singing of 'Auld Lang Syne'. People reflect on the past and make resolutions for the future.

Epiphany (6 January)
Celebrates the revelation to the Gentiles of Jesus Christ as the Saviour, as portrayed by the coming of the Three Wise Men, or Magi. It is the Twelfth Day, traditionally the end of the Christmas season, when all decorations are taken down.

Saraswati Puja (January)
Hindu festival of spring. People dress in sunshine yellow clothes and dance, sing and listen to music.

Chinese New Year (January/February)
The most important Chinese festival lasting 15 days. Families clean and decorate their homes, wear new clothes, and visit their family and friends.

Mardi Gras/Shrove Tuesday (February/March)
Falls on the day before the Christian period of Lent. It literally means 'Fat Tuesday'. People use up certain foods to make pancakes. Celebrations include an elaborate carnival.

A bunch of flowers

What you need
A copy of the photocopiable sheet on page 65 for each child; red, blue, yellow and pink coloured pencils and crayons; scissors; carda large space (inside or outside) for movement; tambourine.

Preparation
Mount the copies of the photocopiable sheet onto card.

What to do
Invite each child to colour their flowers, referring to real examples if possible. Talk about the different names and structures of the flowers and help the children to cut out the cards.

Move to your large space and ask each child to sit in a spot without touching anyone else, and to spread out their cards in front of them. Shake the tambourine gently and explain that this is a signal to move slowly and carefully. Ask the children to walk around the space without touching one another and then to return to their own places. Choose a child to demonstrate how carefully he or she walked. Talk about controlling movements to avoid others.

Next, hit the tambourine loudly and rapidly and explain that this is the signal for moving fast. Divide the group in half and ask each half, in turn, to move as fast as possible around and back again. Draw attention to the children who move with good control.

Let the children spread their flowers out around the space. Make an appropriate signal (slow or fast) and ask different children to go and collect either yellow, blue, red or pink flowers. Repeat to ensure all have a turn, varying the signals and flower colours and sometimes using the flower names for a further challenge.

Finally, ask each child to race and collect one of each flower. Anyone who touches another collector has to stop immediately. The winner is the first child back to their spot with a full bunch.

Support
Limit the flowers to two different kinds only and build up to four over time.

Extension
Let the children play the tambourine and select the flowers to be collected.

Learning objective
To show awareness of space, of themselves and of others.

Group size
Whole group.

Home links
Send the cards home and ask parents and carers to play a simple game. Suggest that they put the cards in different places in the garden or large space, then call out a flower and a way to move, such as hopping or jumping. How fast can their child get to the flower?

Jump for joy!

Learning objective
To move imaginatively with control.

Group size
Ten to twelve children.

What you need
Large hoops; skipping ropes; chalk; beanbags; parcel tape; illustrations of frogs, lambs and horses; a suitable space for jumping games.

What to do
Talk to the group about different animals that jump and ask them to think of as many as possible. Discuss how the animals jump in different ways such as lambs springing upwards, horses running and then jumping, frogs leaping, and so on. Let the group choose different animals, and encourage them to practise jumping like each of these, one at a time.

Next, spread out the hoops around the space and ask each child to sit in one. Ask the children to be frogs jumping from their lily-pads into the water and back again. Invite half the group to demonstrate, while the others watch and look for really good frog-jumps, then swap over. If you have a suitable surface, arrange all the hoops in a line and tape them down to prevent them from sliding. Let the children jump from one hoop to the next to 'frog-jump across the pond'. If you are outside, chalk suitable shapes or weight the hoops with beanbags.

Next, give each child a rope and ask them to make a wiggly line shape with it. Invite them to jump across and along the rope in any way they choose. Let some children demonstrate their ideas. Provide extra challenges by asking them to jump as high, as quickly, slowly, curled up or stretched out as they can. Stop frequently to let the children look at one another, commenting on well-controlled jumps and asking the children to say why they were good. Finish by letting the children move around all the shapes, jumping in a different way for each new rope.

Support
Chalk out, or tape down rope lines. Hold the children's hands to help them jump accurately in and out of the hoops and shapes.

Extension
Introduce some small apparatus such as a gym bench, low blocks or safe climbing apparatus and invite the children to jump over, on and off.

Home links
Ask parents and carers to play 'How far can you run and jump?' in the garden or park. Measure the results for an 'I can long jump … centimetres' chart.

Here we grow!

Learning objective
To move with confidence and imagination in response to an action song.

Group size
Whole group.

What you need
The photocopiable sheet on page 66 enlarged as much as possible; a pointer stick or ruler; a pen.

Preparation
Underline or highlight each action word in the poem.

What to do
Set up the poem where all the children can see it, and read it to them once through, pointing at each word with a pointer. Read it again, asking the children to join in when they can. This time stop at each action word and emphasize it. Give the children an appropriate action to follow or ask them to demonstrate some suggestions of their own.

Go through the poem again, letting the children relish the words and practise the actions. Now ask the children to spread out so that they cannot touch one another. Encourage the group to say the rhyme with you,

making large exaggerated actions to match the words. Then ask the children to pair up and hold hands. Repeat the activity reading out the poem and inviting the children to move as pairs for the actions.

Support
Invite helpers to sit amongst the children to lead with the words and actions, demonstrating what to do. Ask them to partner less confident children if necessary.

Extension
Use the children's suggestions to add another verse or two to the poem. Encourage the children to think of some new actions and to demonstrate these to the rest of the group. Invite them to write down the new verses and to draw the corresponding actions, then ask everyone to move to these together.

The children could also use simple musical instruments and take turns to play an accompaniment to the actions.

Home links
Ask parents and carers to share photographs and memories of their children as they grew up. Suggest that they talk about the things they could do at different ages and what they can do better now.

Don't disturb the tadpoles

What you need
Approximately 20 paper discs about the size of a large dinner plate; parcel tape; skittles or other small objects; card; glue; scissors; blocks; different-sized cardboard boxes; a copy of the photocopiable sheet on page 67 for each child; glue.

Preparation
Set out a short obstacle course around the room using the boxes and blocks. Tape down the paper discs (stepping-stones), ensuring that the path is twisting between the obstacles, the discs being a comfortable child's pace apart. Glue the photocopiable sheets onto card.

What to do
Talk to the children about how frogs lay their frogspawn in ponds. Explain that in springtime the tadpoles will hatch if they are not disturbed.

Provide each child with a photocopiable sheet and invite them to cut out the tadpole cards. Talk about the different cards and how they show the way that a tadpole grows.

Take the children to the 'pond' area and explain that the only way to get across the pond without disturbing the tadpoles is to use the stepping-stones, represented by the paper discs. Tell the children that if they step off a stepping-stone and get their feet wet, they must give up one of their tadpole cards.

Let the children take turns to cross the pond. Then put some skittles or small items in between the stepping-stones to make the crossing more challenging, and invite the children to cross the pond again. Vary the course by asking them to cross the pond starting from the other side or moving backwards!

Support
The children may need a helping hand until they gain confidence. Try putting the stepping-stones closer together to help them.

Extension
Make the course more complicated with fewer stepping-stones (well fastened down) placed further apart, or with slightly larger well-spaced stepping-stones which require some jumps to reach. Ask the children to design the stepping-stone course for one another, or add new challenges by making them go forwards and backwards several times.

Rabbit chase

What you need
A copy of the photocopiable sheet on page 68 for each child; thin card; felt-tipped pens or coloured pencils; scissors; glue; counters.

Preparation
Glue the photocopiable sheets securely onto thin card.

What to do
Explain to the children that they are going to play a game of 'Rabbit chase' but that they need to make their dice first. Give each child a sheet and read together – '1, 2, 3, 4, 5', saying 'rabbit' when looking at the illustration.

Ask each child to carefully colour in the numbers and illustration on their sheet. Then invite them to cut out the template, fold back the flaps, fold along the lines and then glue the template into a cube shape to make a dice.

When the dice are dry, you are ready to play the game. Place a mound of counters in the middle of the table. Each child takes a turn to roll their own dice. If it lands on a number, all the children must try to guess it and show the corresponding number of fingers. If the thrower can match the number correctly, they may take a counter from the pile. If the dice lands on the rabbit, all the children must shout out the word 'rabbit' – the first one to call out gets a bonus counter. The child with the most counters wins!

Support
Enlarge the photocopiable sheet to make the colouring of the template easier, then help the children to cut out the shapes and fold the flaps. Construct the dice for them, using sticky tape to seal the sides.

Extension
After the children have played the game a few times, ask them to play or invent new games using the same dice. For example, give each child ten counters and ask them to count out the right number of counters to match their throw (six for a rabbit).

Learning objective
To manipulate small objects with control.

Group size
Up to eight children.

Home links
Send home some dice games, such as *Snakes and Ladders* and *Ludo*, and ask parents and carers to play these with their children.

Spruce up the house

Learning objective
To handle tools, objects and equipment with increasing control.

Group size
Two or three children.

What you need
A small cardboard box for each child (shoebox or similar); wallpaper samples; a packet of paste (check that this contains no fungicide and is safe for children, or use an alternative adhesive); water; bowl; large pasting brushes; cloth; catalogues and magazines; child-safe scissors.

What to do
Explain to the children that people often want to decorate their homes and freshen up their houses in springtime. Ask each child how their bedroom is decorated at the moment and how they would like it to look next time they decorate it. Together, look at the different wallpaper samples and discuss the colours, patterns and designs. Invite the children to decide which ones might suit bedrooms, kitchens, bathrooms and so on.

Give the children the boxes, with the open side towards them, and explain to them that they are going to make and decorate rooms, using the wallpaper samples. If you are using packet paste, let the group help you make up the glue, reading out the instructions to them. While the paste thickens, let the children choose their wallpaper pieces and help them to push them into their boxes, creasing the edges so that they fit. Help each child to cut the piece to size and then paste it carefully in place.

When all the walls of the boxes are covered, invite each child to cut out magazine pictures of windows, doors, furniture, carpets and occupants to stick onto the walls of their box and complete the room.

Support
Use larger boxes, which are easier to work with. Pre-cut a range of papers to fit the boxes and help the children to check which ones are the right size before pasting.

Extension
Copy out in large letters the instructions that are on the paste packet. Read them together and check the correct order with the children, following the instructions for making the paste. Invite each child to make a label, such as 'This is Joseph's bedroom', and fasten it to their box.

Home links
Ask parents and carers to talk about the way they have decorated their rooms at home and why they chose the colours and designs. Invite them to send left-over wallpaper to school.

Haman noises

What you need
A collection of different percussion instruments, one for each child.

What to do
Tell the children that at the festival of Purim, Jewish families go to the synagogue and hear a story about an evil man called Haman. When the story is being read, all the children make as much noise as they can every time they hear Haman's name. Tell or read the story to your group:

'A man called *Haman* was a minister to the King of Persia. *Haman* thought he was very important and he wanted all the people to bow to him. The Jewish people who were living in Persia did not want to bow to *Haman* because they felt they should only worship God. This made *Haman* angry and he persuaded the King to agree to kill all the Jewish people and take their money. Now the King did not know that his wife, Esther, was Jewish and when she heard of this plan she bravely planned to make the King change his mind. She invited the King and *Haman* to a banquet and told the King that she was Jewish. She uncovered *Haman's* evil plans and the King was very angry. The King realized he had been tricked. He saved the Jewish people and ordered that *Haman* be killed instead.'

Now demonstrate the correct way to play each instrument and let the children take turns to play them. Ask the rest of the group to listen carefully and say how each one is played. Is it shaken, beaten, plucked or stroked? Do they have to use their hands, a beater or a stick? Ensure the children hold the instruments correctly and know how to play them. Ask them to practise playing softly and then loudly, in turns and then all together, watching your signal to make loud or soft sounds. Read the story again, emphasizing Haman's name and encouraging the children to play loudly whenever they hear it.

Support
Limit the instruments to drums, tambourines and triangles.

Extension
Use a wider range of instruments and read the story several times alternately asking only those with certain instruments to drown out Haman's name.

Learning objective
To handle instruments with confidence.

Group size
Eight to ten children.

Home links
Send home a copy of a fairy tale or nursery rhyme and ask parents and carers to read it, encouraging their children to make clapping sounds every time they hear a particular name mentioned.

Gift slices

What you need
Packet of plain meringues; large polythene bag; two large blocks of plain chocolate; 12g sultanas; foil; a small tin foil container for each child; plastic bowl and smaller bowl to fit inside; hot water; mixing spoons; cake decorations.

Preparation
Write the ingredients and the recipe out in large letters for reference. Put the different cake decorations into small containers.

What to do
Explain that about 100 years ago young people often had to work away from home but they all tried to go home for Mothering Sunday, bringing presents for their mothers. Tell the children that they are going to make special chocolate slices for Mother's Day gifts.

Show the children the recipe and let them follow the list of ingredients. Talk about where the ingredients come

from, such as meringues being made from whisked egg white and so on. Pour hot water into the larger bowl and warn the children to take care. Put the smaller bowl inside and let them take turns to break the chocolate bars into it and gently stir the mixture until it melts. Tip the meringues into the polythene bag and take turns to crumble them into pea-sized pieces, then add these to the chocolate mixture, stirring carefully. Add the sultanas, a few at a time, until the mixture is stiff but well coated (if it gets too stiff, add a little hot water and stir briskly).

Tip the mixture into the foil containers and help the children to firm it down. Let them choose cake decorations and gently push these into each slice. Put the slices into the fridge to set.

Support
Break the chocolate up and help the children to mix the ingredients. Make up a mixture of soft margarine and icing sugar to coat the slices to make decorating them easier.

Extension
Let the children follow the recipe instructions (with your help if necessary). Help them to put their mixture onto large baking sheets and cut eight slices, and invite them to decorate each one differently.

Growing garden

What you need
A large round foil pie-
dish container for each
child; a collection of
small pebbles, gravel,
moss, twigs, small flowers
and so on (preferably
gathered by the children);
lolly sticks; strong glue;
pictures of gardens.

Preparation
Make an Easter garden
for demonstration
purposes. Cut some lolly
sticks in half, ready to
make crosses.

What to do
Tell the children the story
of Jesus and how he was
crucified and laid to rest
in a garden tomb. Tell
them how, three days
later, his friend Mary saw
him alive. Explain that
many Christians make small Easter
gardens in their churches at Easter time
to remind people of the story of Jesus'
resurrection.

Show the children the garden that
you have prepared and tell them that
you have used moss to make grassy
lawns, gravel for paths, twigs for trees
and small flower heads pushed into
damp moss for flower beds.

If possible, take the children on a
walk outside to collect their own
materials and look at different types of
gardens. Alternatively, show the
children the materials you have
collected and talk about what they
could be used for. Share the garden
pictures to stimulate ideas and let the
children talk about their own gardens if
they have one.

Give each child a foil tray and let
them use the materials to make their

own garden. Encourage them to talk
about what they have used and why.

Finally, give each child three long
and three short lolly sticks and let them
glue these to make three crosses. When
these are dry, let the children stick
them in a group in their Easter garden.
Make a display of the finished gardens
for everyone to admire.

Support
Let the children make their gardens in
the sand tray or in an outside area.
Provide them with larger materials to
construct their Easter garden.

Extension
Invite the children to plan out their
gardens before they start, drawing out
a simple diagram of their ideas. Ask
them to include more features, such as
the tomb with the stone rolled away.

Learning objective
To manipulate small
materials and objects
with increasing
control.

Group size
Six children.

Home links
Let parents and
carers know that their
children are making
miniature gardens
and ask them to visit
a garden centre to
talk about some
features together.
Suggest that they let
their children have a
small garden area of
their own.

Egg hunt

Learning objective
To travel in different
ways on balancing
and climbing
equipment.

Group size
Five or six children.

What you need
A safe spacious area; tunnels; benches; boxes and/or climbing equipment; table-cloths; mats; 20 paper egg shapes cut out of Post-it notes with the adhesive edge left intact.

Preparation
Set up a small obstacle course using a mixture of large play equipment which will require the children to climb and balance. Make fixed climbing equipment more exciting by fastening table-cloths over sections to form a cover or temporary blocked way. Fix the paper eggs to different areas, underneath and on top of sections so that the children have to work hard to find them.

What to do
Explain to the children that in many countries, on Easter Sunday, adults hide small Easter eggs around their houses and gardens for their children to find. The eggs are a sign of new life in spring and a reminder that Jesus came back to life after dying.

Tell the children that there are paper eggs hidden amongst the apparatus and that they are going to hunt for these by climbing through the equipment. Ask the first child to go along the course, carefully telling them which direction to go and asking them to find two eggs. Invite everyone to watch and suggest where the child is to look. Let all the children take turns until all the eggs are collected. As each child moves, discuss with the whole group how they are moving. Are they climbing, balancing, going under, over or through?

Next, ask the children to go through the course in the reverse direction, this time hiding some of their eggs for others to find. Repeat the activity when all the eggs have been hidden again.

Support
Keep the course on a fairly low level and hang the paper eggs on strings so that the children have to stretch up high. Give them a hand to support them.

Extension
Put numbers on the eggs and see who can get the highest total. Make the course more challenging so that children really have to search – literally high and low – for the eggs!

Home links
Ask parents and carers to carefully blow eggs (make a small hole in either end and shake the egg out) and decorate them with their children. Hang the eggs on an Easter tree in your setting.

Court jesters

What you need
Felt in bright colours; a wooden spoon or spatula for each child; strong glue; scissors; a tiny sew-on bell for each child; sequins; felt-tipped pens; scraps of ribbon about 30cm long; card or plastic triangle-shaped templates (sides about 4cm long); a jar to hold the drying 'Fools'.

Preparation
Make a mini 'Fool' to show the children before the activity.

What to do
Explain to the children that on 1 April – April Fools' Day – many people play jokes on each other and that, after midday, the joke is on the joker! Talk with the children about things that make them laugh.

Explain that a long time ago there was a special job of 'Fool' or 'Court jester', when men wore bright, outrageous clothes with bells on and made people laugh. The jesters often carried a miniature 'Fool' to wave at people when they teased them. Show the children your prepared 'Fool' and explain that they are going to make one of these.

Provide each child with a wooden spoon or spatula and let them draw a face on the inside of it. Then let them cut out about eight felt triangle shapes using the templates. Help them to stick these onto the outside and rim of the spoon, leaving the top tips sticking up to make the points of a hat. Encourage them to stick on sequins to the tips. Help them to wind ribbon around the neck of their spoon and to thread the tiny bell onto this, so that it can ring when waved. Stand all the children's 'Fools' upright in a jar to dry, then let the children use them as puppets.

Support
Pre-cut the triangles for the children and have the ribbons and bells already fixed onto the spoons.

Extension
Let the children draw out their own triangle shapes of different sizes. Encourage each child to use felt scraps to make a collage face and to add a decorated fabric cloak around the handle of the spoon.

Learning objective
To use tools and small equipment with confidence.

Group size
Three or four children.

Home links
Ask parents and carers to send in jokes for their children to share with the whole group.

Learning objective
To use a range of
small equipment with
confidence.

Group size
Eight to ten children.

New flags

What you need
A copy of the photocopiable sheet on page 69 for each child; yellow and black felt-tipped pens or bright colouring pencils or crayons; pencils; a ball of string; glue; paper clips; thin card.

Preparation
Glue the photocopiable sheets onto thin card. Find a suitable fixing point for the flags to hang at right-angles to a wall.

What to do
Tell the children that at Baisakhi, Sikhs remember how five courageous volunteers were willing to sacrifice themselves to show how much they cared for their beliefs. However, it was just a test devised by their leader Guru Gobind Singh to find brave followers who became a special group, or Khalsa. To celebrate this event each year, Sikhs put up a new yellow and black flag at their Gurdwara (known as the Nishan Sahib). The black Khanda sign of crossed swords is a reminder that the Khalsa were ready to die and defend their religion.

Give each child a photocopiable sheet and let them cut out the flag shape and carefully colour it in yellow and the Khanda black. Show them how to fold over the short left-hand edge and cover it with glue. Unwind a long length of string and help each child to fasten their

flag around it. Clip each flag on with paper clips to hold it firmly until the glue dries. Once all the flags are in place, fasten the string from a high point in the room to hang down a wall. Ensure that the points of the flags stand out at

right angles to the wall, just as one single flag would be at a Gurdwara.

Support
Enlarge the photocopiable sheet and let the children make larger flags.

Extension
Invite each child to cover a plain flag shape with yellow fabric scraps. Then let them colour in the black Khanda from a photocopiable sheet, and help them to cut it out very carefully, sticking it onto the yellow background. Help the children to fasten their flags to sticks as individual Nishan Sahibs.

St George and the dragon

What you need
A large space; a large safety-pin for each child; sticky tape; two red PE bands; a copy of the photocopiable sheet on page 70 for each child; felt-tipped pens or coloured pencils; scissors; card.

Preparation
Glue the photocopiable sheets onto card.

What to do
Give each child a photocopiable sheet and let them cut out the emblem and colour the dragon in red, yellow, blue or green. Help each child to tape their dragon badge to a large safety pin and then fasten it safely to their T-shirt or top.

Warm-up by inviting the children to move around the area as angry/sleepy/little/fast/big or slow dragons according to your commands! Choose a child to be St George and let him or her put on crossed PE bands. Check that all the children know the colour of their dragon badges by asking those with each different colour to sit or stand in turn. Call out one colour and invite the corresponding children to run around the space without touching anyone else, while all the other children sit still on the floor. St George chases the dragons and as each one is touched on the arm they must stop and hold up one arm above their head. Repeat the activity, letting the children take turns to be St George and altering the dragon colour groups.

Vary the activity by asking the children to move in different ways, such as crawling, hopping, jumping and so on. Throughout the activity, stress the need to move without bumping into anyone or anything!

Invite the group to cool down by standing as tall as possible and being huge sleepy dragons – gradually sinking down and curling up tightly to sleep. Repeat several times and then let the children rest quietly, curled up, for a few minutes.

Support
Choose only two dragons to be chased at a time. Hold hands with 'St George' and help him or her to chase the dragons.

Extension
Have two or three 'St Georges' so that the children have to really look around carefully as they move.

Learning objective
To move and use space with confidence.

Group size
Ten to fifteen children.

Home links
Ask parents and carers to play 'Tag' with their children at home. Suggest that they vary the way all the players move – hopping, walking, running backwards and so on.

Learning objective
To move with control
and co-ordination.

Group size
Six to eight children.

Home links
Ask parents and
carers to play 'I Spy the
wind moving the…'
and to see how many
things are blown by
moving air. Send a
photocopiable sheet
home with each child
and ask them to play
the fish-flapping
game with their
family.

Fish in a flap!

What you need
A copy of the photocopiable sheet on
page 71 for each child; felt-tipped pens
or colouring materials; scissors; a
folded sheet of newspaper for each
child; chalk; a large space.

What to do
Explain that in Japan, fish, especially
carp, are a sign of strength and energy
and are used for lanterns and games for
Children's Day. The Japanese use the
fish as a symbol and encouragement
for children to grow up strong,
energetic and healthy.
   Invite each child to colour and cut out
the fish shape from their photocopiable
sheet. Give them a folded newspaper,
then ask them to find a space and put
their fish on the floor in front of them.
Demonstrate how to flap the newspaper
down towards the floor to make the fish
lift and move along. Let the children
practise this, flapping gently then
strongly. Discuss which sort of flapping
works the most effectively. What makes

the fish move along? What other things
are moved by the wind or air moving
(such as leaves, washing, windmills,
balloons and so on)?
   Let the children stand in a row, and
chalk a finishing line in front of them.
When you say 'Go!', invite them to flap
their fish in a race to see who can cross
the line first. Next, chalk a wavy line in
front of each child and repeat the
activity, encouraging each child to
make the fish go along the line, seeing
who can control them and reach the
end first.

Support
Chalk a circular fish pond and stand the
children around it, but a little way from
it, letting them take turns to flap their
fish into the 'water'.

Extension
Put the children into small relay teams
and invite them to flap their fish up to
a line and back, passing the newspaper
to the next child to take his or her turn.

Fun in the sun

What you need
A collection of: sun-hats, sun-glasses, suncream bottles, adult-sized T-shirts, coats, umbrellas, wellington boots, scarves and gloves.

Preparation
Make large signs with sun, rain and snow pictures on them.

What to do
Talk about the sun and what happens if people stay too long in the sun, as well as how we can enjoy the sun safely. Discuss sunburn, using sun-glasses, sun-hats, sitting in the shade and using suncream. Encourage the children to talk about their holidays and how their families keep them protected from too much sun.

Show the children your collection of items and ask them to say which should be used in which weather conditions. Hold up, one by one, the weather pictures that you have prepared and ask the children, in turn, to choose one item appropriate for the condition and wear it or pretend to use it. Ask the others to say if they agree or not, and why. Each time the sun sign is used, emphasize the importance of the chosen item. Ask questions such as, 'Why do we need a sun-hat?', 'What does suncream do?' and so on. Repeat the exercise, this time asking the children to wear two or three things to match the weather sign.

Finish by having races, asking two children at a time to dress for the weather sign and see who is ready first!

Support
Limit the items to a small collection (such as sun-hat, sun-glasses and suncream; umbrella, wellington boots and coat) and have only a rain and sun sign.

Extension
Invite the children to make a poster entitled 'To keep safe in the sun we need to…'. Ask them to draw colourful pictures of themselves wearing appropriate protection. Let them write or copy explanatory labels such as 'Sit in the shade'.

Learning objective
To raise health awareness of the dangers of too much sun.

Group size
Eight to ten children.

Home links
Let parents and carers know that you are covering safety in the sun. Ask them to talk to their children about it at home. Encourage them to send in sun-hats to wear during outdoor play sessions. Display the older children's sun safety poster in a prominent place for parents to see.

Where are the minibeasts?

Learning objective
To handle tools safely and with increasing control.

Group size
Eight to ten children.

Home links
Send home books with pictures of minibeasts and a small logbook (made of a few stapled sheets of paper). Ask parents and carers to help their children to make a few days' entries of all the minibeasts they have seen and where. Display and share the books together.

What you need
A copy of the photocopiable sheet on page 72 for each child; scissors; glue.

Preparation
Take the children on a minibeast hunt around your setting, turning over leaves and stones and looking at trees and shrubs. Ensure that you replace turned-over stones and logs in their exact positions.

What to do
Remind the children about what they found on their minibeast hunt outside. Talk about how different small insects and creatures live in a variety of places. Give each child a photocopiable sheet and talk about the picture together.

Then talk about the minibeasts at the bottom of the sheet. Invite the children to name them and say where the creatures might hide on the picture. Ask them to cut out each minibeast and carefully stick it where they think it might live on the picture. Encourage each child to explain to the others why they have chosen their particular places.

Support
Enlarge the sheets to make the cutting and sticking easier.

Extension
Ask the children to complete simple sentences to explain where their insects are hiding, such as 'My ant is hiding under a leaf'.

Summer salad

What you need

Two very different lettuces; tomatoes; cucumber; peppers; cress; any other unusual salad ingredients (such as chicory); olive oil; salad vinegar; colander; salad spinner; chopping boards; knives; two large salad bowls; small jug; knives and forks; salad servers; plates; access to a sink or bowl of clean water.

What to do

Invite everyone to wash their hands carefully and stress the importance of hygiene. Let the children wash the lettuces and put them into the spinner, taking turns to operate the handle. Ask them what they think will happen inside. Show them how the water has been spun off.

Divide the lettuce between the two large salad bowls. Suggest that the children take turns to wash the other ingredients, using a colander to drain off the water. Ask if this is better than a spinner and why.

Show the children the peppers and ask them what is inside. Cut off the tops and show them the seeds, warning them not to eat them. Demonstrate how to cut the other ingredients on the chopping boards and let each child try, always stressing the safety aspects of using knives. Let the children divide the ingredients between the two bowls and take turns to mix the salad, using the salad servers. Encourage them to talk about the different colours and textures and tell you how they make an interesting salad mixture.

Explain that many people enjoy a dressing on their salad to give it more flavour. Use the jug and let the children add a little oil and vinegar, mixing it together in turns. Help them to pour it over one bowl and toss it thoroughly, asking what is happening to the salad. Then let them serve the plain salad to the group and talk about tastes, textures, likes and dislikes. Repeat, using the tossed salad. Make a tally of which salad was preferred.

Support

Pre-cut the tomatoes and any other difficult-to-cut items.

Extension

Encourage the children to draw and label diagrams of how to make a salad and use tools safely. Act as scribe where necessary.

By the seaside

Learning objective
To handle tools and objects with control.

Group size
Two or three children.

What you need
Sand tray or large container of wet sand; small rakes; spades and trowels; small moulds and buckets; cocktail sticks; adhesive address labels; coloured felt-tipped pens; pictures of the seaside; a range of shells and small pebbles.

Preparation
Make flags by sticking two address labels together and fastening them onto cocktail sticks. Make about four for each child.

children feel the sand and try pressing it together to make a shape. Explain that the dampness makes the sand cling to itself and ask what dry sand might do.

Invite the children to work together to build the largest sand-castle they can, decorating it with shells and pebbles. As the children work, stop and discuss their building and how they have made it. When it is nearly completed, show them the blank flags and encourage them to draw their own

What to do
Talk about families going to the seaside in summer. Ask children who have played on the beach to tell the group what they have seen, heard, touched and smelled. Look at the pictures of the seaside together and discuss the different things that are going on – stressing that the weather needs to be warm for children to wear beach clothes and play on the sand.

Talk about sand-castles and demonstrate how to press wet sand into a small bucket or mould, reverse it and tap the bottom, gently removing the shaper to reveal the castle. Let the

to add to the castle. If possible, take a photo of their final castle for a display.

Support
Let the children build their own castles allowing them more space. Try tipping damp sand onto plastic table-cloths for the children to work on.

Extension
Invite the children to draw out designs for their castle before they begin. Ask them to use the flags to label different parts of their castle, saying what happens there. Act as scribe, or let them copy words from a list they suggest.

Home links
Ask parents and carers to take their children for a trip to the seaside or to a castle or simply to play in a sandpit together at a local park.

Me and my shadow

What you need
A large space, outside and on a sunny day!

What to do
Take the children to a large space where they can clearly see shadows. Explain how the sun shines down, but that shadows are formed when the sun is blocked by a solid object like a person's body. Invite the children to stand in a safe space with their backs to the sun (or light source if you have to be inside). Ask them to look at their shadows, raising one arm. Encourage them to raise different combinations of arms and legs and look at their shadows. Then ask each child to make a shadow shape of their choice. Stop and let the children look at one another's patterns and shapes.

Now let the children warm up by running, jumping or hopping as you direct, to see if they can escape from their shadows! Talk about how the shapes change, but never go away as long as the sun or a bright light shines on them. Next, ask the children to pair up and see what different shapes they can make as shadows (stretching up, curling and so on). Compare and talk about the different shapes they have made. Then explain that they can pretend to be shadows. Let them stay in pairs and ask one child to stand behind another. Invite the front child to put an arm up and ask the 'shadow' to put the same arm up. Let the front child change his shape and the second child shadow the movement. Ask half the group to work so the others can observe. Talk about how the 'shadow' must follow the leader exactly. Change roles and repeat the activity.

Support
Work in smaller groups and have one leader. Help the whole group to act as shadows and guide them to make the same shapes.

Extension
Let each child work out a simple series of shadow moves with a partner to make a sequence. Play different types of music and let them make a simple shadow movement dance, repeating their sequences.

Learning objective
To move with confidence, imagination and safety.

Group size
Ten to sixteen children.

Home links
Ask parents and carers to put a large stick in a pot, where the sun shines, and to watch and talk about with their children how the length of the shadow changes at different times of the day.

Weather forecast

Learning objective
To recognize that changes happen to their bodies when they are active.

Group size
Ten to sixteen children.

What you need
A large space; four large sheets of card; Blu-Tack; felt-tipped pens.

Preparation
Draw a suitable weather symbol and matching word for sunshine, rain, wind and cloud – one on each sheet of card.

What to do
Take the children to a large space and talk about the weather forecast they may have seen on television. Show them the sheets and explain what the symbols mean. Talk about what we wear in different weathers during the summer months and what different things we can do – such as playing outside, jumping in puddles, flying a kite or putting on a jacket.

Ask the children to sit down in a safe spot where they cannot touch anyone else. Tell them that you are going to play a slow game and that every time you hold up a card, they must act out an action that matches the symbol, on the spot. Provide some examples and then hold up the signs for the children to have a go.

Fasten the signs, one on each side of the room, and explain to the children that they are going to play a fast game. Carefully rehearse what each sign is and explain that when you say, 'It's sunny!' they must run to the 'sunny' sign as quickly as possible. Let everyone practise this. Call out different signs and let the children race to get to them. When the children are beginning to get out of breath, let them sit down. Ask each child to put their hand on their chest and feel how their heart is beating fast and how heavy their breathing is. Talk about how their hearts beat faster when they move quickly.

Support
Join in the running to the signs with the children and assist them with finding the right direction.

Extension
Invite the children to circle the room before each weather forecast and make the changes of direction more difficult. Add the command 'sunbathing' which requires them to stop still and lie on the floor.

Home links
Ask parents to play running races such as 'Tag' with their children. Suggest that they talk about how their heart beat and breathing change when they are very active.

Tree delights

What you need
A copy of the photocopiable sheet on page 73 for each child; very thick paint; brushes; glue; sequins; beads and glitter; thin ribbons or thick, coloured wool; small branch, set in a pot of earth; thin card; thin plastic bags (optional).

Preparation
Mount the photocopiable sheets onto thin card.

What to do
Talk about how Christmas trees are decorated inside houses as part of Christmas celebrations. Explain to the children that at Wesak, many Buddhists remember the day that Buddha was born, became enlightened and died (all on the same day). They celebrate this happy occasion by decorating their homes and gardens, especially by hanging

decorations in trees – it was under a tree that Buddha reached enlightenment (understanding of all life's meaning and pattern).

Give each child a photocopiable sheet and say that they will make some Wesak tree decorations. Let them cut out the decoration shapes, helping them in particular with the tricky hanging circle sections and the small circle areas. Ask them to paint the shapes thickly with bright colours on both sides, hanging them on the branch to dry. Ask why they have chosen their colours and to say what natural and man-made things are the same colour. Later, invite them to brush glue onto their decorations and to add different coloured glitter and sequins to make sparkling patterns. Ask them which colours will go well with the background they have painted. Let them select ribbons or wool and thread these through the smaller holes. Help them to tie these in place, letting the ends dangle attractively. Hang the decorations onto the branch and display them outside so that the breeze will make the them sway and sparkle in the sun. Staple the hangings into thin transparent plastic bags to make them waterproof if you want to leave them outside.

Support
Cut the decoration templates out for the children or enlarge the photocopiable sheets to make handling easier.

Extension
Encourage the children to create their own decorative hanging shapes, writing on the names of things that they like – such as their friends' or pets' names.

Learning objective
To manipulate tools and objects with increasing control.

Group size
Six to eight children.

Home links
Ask parents and carers to help their children to make a waterproof hanging of their own to bring to your setting and decorate a real tree. Have a special decorating ceremony with drinks and biscuits.

Ladder bread

What you need
Packet of bread mix; large mixing bowl; measuring jug; water; fork; flour; pastry board or clean trays; damp tea towel; pair of clean scissors; baking tray; access to an oven.

What to do
Tell the children that Jewish families, at Shavuot, remember how Moses climbed a high mountain and received the Ten Commandments from God. Explain that the Ten Commandments were rules on how to live a good life. At Shavuot, synagogues are decorated with fruit and flowers. After the service, families go home for a special meal, where they eat 'Ladder bread'. This bread has a ladder pattern on it to remind everyone of how Moses had to climb a mountain to talk to God.

Ask the children to wash their hands thoroughly. Make the bread mix up as directed, adding water and letting the children take turns to mix and then knead the mixture. Help them shape two thirds of the dough into a lozenge shape and then roll the remainder into a fat sausage. Show the children how to use the scissors to cut this into eight pieces. Roll these pieces into smaller sausage shapes and then press them into the loaf top in a slanting pattern (like an ear of corn) to make the ladder. Dust the loaf with flour and leave it under a damp towel until it has risen to double its size (about 30 minutes). Then ask the children what has happened and explain that the yeast has made the bread rise. Bake as directed in a hot oven. Share the loaf together when it has cooled down and retell the story of Moses and the Ten Commandments.

Support
Divide the kneaded dough into four sections and help the children to make individual 'Ladder bread' rolls.

Extension
Let the children draw out picture instructions to show how to make 'Ladder bread'. Act as their scribe, adding any text that they want.

Ladder bread

High summer

What you need
A large space; a pair of sun-glasses and a sun-hat for each child.

What to do
Explain that around Midsummer's Day, the hours of light and sunshine are at their longest and that the sun is at its strongest of the year. Tell the children that they are going to play a game together. Invite them to find a space to lie down where they cannot touch anyone else. Ask them to imagine that they are in bed, waking up slowly as the sun rises. Talk about the things they might do – stretching, washing, getting dressed – and let them perform these movements. Invite half the group to demonstrate and ask the others to watch and try to guess what is happening. Repeat the activity, changing the groups. Next, ask the children to imagine that they are going for a walk, doing different things in the sunshine. Encourage them to use the whole space available. Stop and let different children demonstrate their ideas for the others to copy. Now encourage the children to think of slow, fast, big and small movements and then to put several different movements together. Then ask them to move back to another safe space and move as if they are getting ready for bed. Repeat the sequences.

Finally, put a pile of sun-hats and sunglasses in the middle of the space. Tell the children that when you say

'sunrise' they must mime some getting-up movements, and when you say 'sunset' they must mime some bedtime movements, but when you say 'high summer' they must put on a hat and glasses as quickly as they can. Incorporate these phrases into a story about a child going through the day doing different things. Repeat the activity several times, encouraging the children to use the whole space safely.

Support
Limit the dressing-up to sun-hats, gradually introducing the sun-glasses over time.

Extension
Add more instructions such as 'mid-morning' and 'tea-time' to encourage the children to listen, think and respond with more challenge.

Learning objective
To move with imagination, confidence and safety.

Group size
Ten to fifteen children.

Home links
Ask parents and carers to play timed races of getting up and getting ready for bed to encourage swifter dressing and undressing!

Key surprise

Learning objective
To use tools and wood safely and with increasing control.

Group size
Two to three children.

Home links
Ask parents and carers to send in wood off-cuts and tools and materials to set up a woodworking area. Ask them to play a game at home – looking at different types of key for different locks such as house, car, garage, cupboard and so on.

What you need
A selection of small, differently shaped wood off-cuts; table; medium quality sandpaper sheets; pencils; hammer; large nails; hanging tabs and small tacks (to fasten these); thick paint mixed with PVA adhesive; brushes; sticky tape.

Preparation
Make a key rack to show the children.

What to do
Explain that Father's Day is a recent custom to thank fathers for their love and care. Show the children the different wood off-cuts and tell them that they will make a key rack for Daddy's keys. Remain sensitive to the children's circumstances and, if appropriate, invite them to make their gifts for other significant males in their lives instead.

Let each child choose a piece of wood. Talk about splinters and safety and show them how to use a piece of sandpaper to smooth over any rough edges – explain how the rough surface smooths the wood. Let the children choose a colour and paint over the wood, leaving it to dry in a warm place.

When the wood is dry, talk about how many keys can hang on the racks. Ask the children where they would like to have the nails, letting them mark the places with a pencil. Demonstrate how to hold a long nail by the shaft and use a hammer safely. Help them to tap the nails into place. Talk about where the hanging tab needs to be to make the rack hang straight, emphasizing the need for balance. Tape the hanging tab into place (letting the large nails hang over the edge of a table) and help the children to gently hammer the fixing tacks in the holes. Pull off the tape and let the children test out the key rack.

Support
Use regular off-cut shapes (such as squares and rectangles) and sand the edges before use.

Extension
Let the children copy the words 'Daddy's keys' using a fine brush or felt-tipped pens.

Flaming messages

What you need
Large clear space; bench or climbing box; hoops; rope; skittles; a copy of the photocopiable sheet on page 74 for each child; scissors; glue; red and gold glitter; card signs saying 'over, under, round and through'; sticky tape; thin card.

Preparation
Mount the photocopiable sheets onto thin card. In a large space, set up an obstacle course with a bench or box (attach the 'over' sign), one or two hoops (labelled 'through'), a rope – to be held up by helpers or fixed to uprights (labelled 'under') and skittles in a ring (labelled 'around').

What to do
Explain to the children that Pentecost is celebrated by Christians to remember how God sent flames which rested on the disciples' heads. Give each child a photocopiable sheet and let them cut out the flame shape. Invite them to cover this with glue and then sprinkle gold and red glitter onto the shapes to make glowing flames. Leave the pictures to dry.

Show the children the obstacle course and demonstrate how they will go through the course, stopping at each label and reading it together. Let each child, in turn, practise travelling along the course. Now split the group into two, putting children at either end of the course. Give each child their golden flame and ask them to carry it along the course to take their message to the other end, handing it to the child they meet at that end of the course who then lays the flame down. This receiving child then carries their own flame back along the course and hands it to the child at the far end, who puts it safely down. Continue until all the children have completed the course.

Swap the groups over to the other end of the course. Let them return along the course empty-handed in turn, each child collecting their own flame from the pile at the opposite end.

Support
Help the children to move along the course, holding their hands if necessary, and reading out the signs for them.

Extension
Make a more complex course by adding more than one hoop, climbing-over section and so on, to make the process more difficult for the children.

Learning objective
To travel under, over, around and through equipment.

Group size
Ten to fifteen children.

Home links
Ask parents and carers to help their children to look out for things that you go under, over, around and through.

Learning objective
To move in a team
and use space with
confidence.

Group size
Fifteen children or
more.

Racing boats

What you need
A three-metre length of wide brightly coloured ribbon or band braid per team of five children (preferably a different colour for each team); large clear space; three marker skittles for each team; drum and beater.

around the skittle and back home without dropping hands. Beat the drum to set the pace of movement, just like the drummer in a dragon boat does to encourage the rowers. Repeat, this time with each team joining hands in a line (no overtaking allowed). Practise this until the children can show good control in a team. Then give each team their dragon boat ribbon and ask them to hold onto part of it, one at each end with others spaced along the length. This time, let them walk around holding the 'boat' as you beat the rhythm. Repeat, beating out a faster rhythm, letting them move as quickly as possible holding on to the 'boat'.

What to do
Explain that Chinese people enjoy a race with long boats for their Dragon Boat Festival. Put the children into teams of five and invite them to sit in straight lines. Put a skittle a few metres ahead of each team and let each child, in turn, stand up, walk around the skittle and return to their place. Repeat, but this time ask each child to run round the same course. See who can do this first, but praise all those who complete the race successfully.

Ask the children to stand up and join hands. Tell them that the whole team has to work together now to complete the course. Encourage them to walk

Finally, add two extra skittles to the course and challenge the children to walk and then race in between all the markers.

Support
Let the children race in pairs, holding each end of a shorter, or doubled-up, loop of ribbon. Restrict the course to two skittles.

Extension
Let the children race around more skittles, racing both forwards and backwards. Invite them to paint dragons' heads to carry at the front of the dragon boat teams.

Heave-ho!

What you need
Long rope; brightly coloured scarf; chalk; sticky tape; clear, safe space; floor mats.

Preparation
Find the middle of the rope and mark it with a piece of tape.

how to 'take the strain' (hold the rope in tension) and gently pull against one another until the scarf comes over to a chalk mark. Warn them not to let the rope slide through their hands to prevent rope burns, and explain that the pull has to be steady and strong, not jerky. Ask them what they think the

What to do
Explain that children often celebrate the feast of O'bon by playing 'Tug-of-war' games. Tell the children that this is also a traditional British competition and is often played as a country sport.

Show the children the rope with the sticky tape in the middle and tell them that they are going to play a version of 'Tug-of-war'. Ask them to help you tie the scarf around the middle mark, leaving the ends dangling. Lie the rope on the floor and make two chalk marks, one each side – about 20cm from the marker. Put floor mats right up to the chalk marks. Ask two children to hold the rope on opposite sides, sitting behind the chalk marks. Demonstrate how to hold the rope securely, then

best way to pull and hold position is and tell them they should sit for best effect. Invite another pair to 'tug' and repeat the discussions. Let every pair have a turn and then repeat the 'Tug-of-war' with two children pulling against another pair, building up the size of the teams until all the children are on one side or the other.

Support
Let the children compete in pairs only and invite helpers to take the anchor position behind them to keep the rope in a safe position.

Extension
Let the children stand for the activity. Stress the safety factors and make sure there are mats over the floor area.

Floral designs

What you need
Different-coloured pieces of Plasticine or play dough; modelling boards; modelling tools; threading lace for each child; examples of different fallen summer flowers; a copy of the photocopiable sheet on page 75 for each child; thin card.

Preparation
Mount the photocopiable sheets onto thin card.

What to do
Explain to the group that Hindu families often pray to Ganesh, the wise elephant-headed god, when they have a problem to solve or if they are making a new start like moving house or getting married. They often have little models of Ganesh in their houses and to celebrate his festival they like to make pretty garlands of flowers to hang round.

Give each child a photocopiable sheet and ask them to cut out Ganesh, placing him on their modelling board. Look carefully together at the flowers you have collected and talk about the colour, size, perfume, number of petals and so on. Ask the children to use the Plasticine or play dough to make a selection of small flowers in varying colours for a garland to fit around Ganesh's neck. Suggest that they make the petals and fit them together to make each flower.

When the flowers are made, let the children arrange them in a garland pattern on their boards. Talk about the designs they have made and if they are the right size. Let them make any adjustments which are necessary to improve their designs.

Finally, help each child to thread the flowers on a lace and carefully wrap it around Ganesh's neck. Make a display of all the Ganesh decorations.

Support
Enlarge the photocopiable sheet and restrict the number of Plasticine or play-dough colours.

Extension
Let the children design repeating patterns in their garlands and add labels to name the different flowers they have used. Challenge them to design a means of making Ganesh stand up for the display.

Digging deep

What you need
Area of garden; garden spades; forks; trowels; a collection of different bulbs – daffodils, tulips, hyacinths and snowdrops; illustrations of the flowers in bloom; lolly sticks; marker pens.

What to do
Explain that in autumn, people plant bulbs which will gradually grow through the winter months and bloom in the spring when the weather becomes warmer. Go to your area of garden with the children and demonstrate how to use the tools, showing the children how to loosen and remove weeds, stacking them in a pile. Let the children take turns to prepare the garden patch by digging it over and clearing away any weeds. Discuss how best to dig and turn the earth, and let them feel their hearts beating faster.

Show the children the bulbs, stressing that bulbs should never be eaten. Invite them to sort the bulbs by size and look at the pictures of the flowers, compare their size and height.

Let the children decide where they would like each flower to bloom, explaining that in nature, they often grow in clumps together. Show them how to use a trowel to dig a hole and plant a bulb with root parts downwards. Encourage the children to take turns to plant the bulbs and cover them with soil.

Finally, help each child to write their name on one side of a lolly stick with the name of the bulb on the other. Plan regular visits to the garden over the winter and into the spring to note and talk about what is happening.

Support
Prepare the lolly sticks with the bulb names and add faint outlines of the children's own names for them to go over. Help each child to plant two contrasting bulbs.

Extension
Let the children make a large plan of the garden area and mark where they have planted a bulb, writing in the name of the flower.

Learning objective
To move with control and co-ordination.

Group size
Six to eight children.

Home links
Send each child home with a daffodil bulb, a small flower pot and growing instructions. Ask parents and carers to help their children to plant and watch it grow on a window sill.

Autumn walk

Learning objective
To move with confidence, imagination and safety.

Group size
Up to thirteen (more if sufficient adult helpers).

What you need
Open space with plenty of fallen leaves; notebook; pen.

What to do
Ask the children to bring in wellington boots or old shoes and tell them to dress warmly, including gloves. Talk about appropriate clothes for autumn days and keeping dry and snug. Explain

that they are going on a walk outdoors and that they need to look, listen and smell all the signs of autumn. Stress the need to keep together and talk about road safety (if leaving your setting).

As you come across fallen leaves, let the children scrunch through them. Discuss the sound of the leaves and ask how they are different from leaves in summer. In a safe open place, let them gather leaves together in large piles and then encourage them to take turns to kick them as high in the air as they can.

Put the children into small teams and let them have two minutes to see which team can make the biggest pile.

Now play some games with the children – start with 'Follow-my-leader', leading the way between all the piles, altering your speed and inviting the children to copy your actions. Choose different children to act as leader in turn and repeat the activity. Next, see who can collect the most different-coloured leaves in a few timed minutes. Vary this by asking for the biggest/ smallest/crunchiest/ brightest coloured leaf. Let each child collect their favourite leaf to take back with them for a display.

Finally, ask the children to stand silently for one minute, to listen and remember what they have heard, then sniff deeply to describe what they can smell. Tell them to remove their gloves and talk about the feel of the leaves. Let them take turns to make suggestions and note their ideas to add to a display.

Support
Invite parents, carers and helpers to join the team games and races to encourage the children.

Extension
Make an autumn collage about the walk. Let the children stick on the leaves they have found and ask them to add drawings of themselves with speech bubbles containing their thoughts on the walk.

Home links
Ask parents and carers to remind their children of road safety and sensible dressing for the autumn months.

Dark nights

What you need
Safe space – preferably in a corner position; climbing frame or collection of secure screens and large boxes; blocks; several large lengths of dark-coloured fabric; string; sticky tape; safety-pins; pictures of squirrels, mice and hedgehogs; torch.

Preparation
If necessary, screw cup hooks (safely above the children's height) and hang lengths of string from them to help the children fasten the fabric.

What to do
Talk to the children about how it gets dark earlier in autumn as winter approaches and the sun is further away from our part of the Earth. Explain how some animals find safe places to hibernate and sleep through the cold, dark months of the year. Show the children the animal pictures and talk about where they might hibernate.

Explain to the children that they are going to make a hibernation den big enough for all the group to play in, using all the materials and equipment you show them. Ask them for ideas of how they might build it, looking at all the available materials and fixing points together. Let them experiment with building, helping them to fix any difficult sections. Encourage the children to share their ideas, asking them questions to stimulate their imagination, such as, 'Is it a safe place to hide and hibernate in?', 'Is it dark enough?', 'Where will you store your food?' and so on. Encourage the children to collect any resources they need from your setting to complete their den.

Finally, let the children get inside and use the torch in turns. Encourage them to role-play inside the den and talk about light, dark and shadows.

Support
Help the children by fixing one large length of fabric over the top of the frame or area to make it dark in advance. Let them complete the den themselves.

Extension
Let the children design and make animal masks to wear as they play in their hibernation den.

Learning objective
To use a range of small and large equipment.

Group size
About four children.

Home links
Ask parents and carers to talk with their children about keeping safe on dark days. Encourage the wearing of reflective arm bands or carrying torches in rural areas.

Foggy day

Learning objective
To move with control and confidence.

Group size
Six to eight children.

What you need
Safe, open space (inside or outside); skittles; ropes; scarf.

What to do
Ask the children if they have seen fog or mist and let them share any experiences they may have had. Talk about how sometimes in autumn, as days become colder, thick fog makes it difficult to see very far.

Explain to the children that they are going to play a foggy-day game. Set out a rope in a curved shape and encourage the children to take turns to walk slowly along it, following it carefully. Blindfold volunteers with the scarf and demonstrate how to lead each one gently along the shaped rope. Invite the children to take turns at leading and following.

Next, set out the skittles to form an easy straight-line obstacle course. Blindfold another child and demonstrate how to lead them through the skittles, zigzagging between alternate skittles. Encourage the children to take turns, firstly with you leading them, and then in pairs, with a leader and follower.

Support
Use only a few skittles and act as the children's leader through the course.

Extension
Let the children design a simple obstacle course. Talk about left and right directions and then let them give instructions to one another such as: 'Two steps left, one right...' as they go along the course.

Home links
Ask parents and carers to let their children look out of the windows early in the morning and at bedtime to look for any signs of fog or mist. Ask them to talk about things they can see clearly and how street lighting helps people to move safely.

Squirrel hunt

What you need
Large clear space; a copy of the photocopiable sheet on page 76 for each child; a lolly stick for each child; scissors; sticky tape; brown and grey felt-tipped pens or crayons; illustrations of red and grey squirrels; firm card.

Preparation
Mount the photocopiable sheets onto firm card.

What to do
Talk to the children about squirrels hibernating in winter and preparing their stores of nuts during autumn. Show the children pictures of grey and red squirrels and explain to them that red squirrels are much rarer than grey ones. Talk about the pictures together, commenting on the squirrels' bushy tails, their bright eyes and their sharp teeth and claws that help them to open nuts.

Give each child a photocopiable sheet and ask them to colour their squirrel

either grey or brown-red. Let them cut out their squirrel carefully and help them to tape a small stick to it, leaving a handle to hold.

Move to a clear space with the children and explain that they are going on a hunt for nuts and that they must make the appropriate actions using their squirrel stick puppets. Let each child find a space away from everyone else and remind them that they must not touch anyone else. Then tell them the squirrels' hunt tale (below), encouraging the children to use their squirrel puppets to demonstrate the actions.

'In the trees the squirrels wake up. No nuts!
They search the branches hopping along. No nuts!
They circle the tree trunks. No nuts!
They reach up to the tree tops. No nuts!
They jump down to the ground. No nuts!
They search through the fallen leaves on the ground. No nuts!
Then they crawl under the roots and dig in the soil. Here are the nuts!'

Practise the different movements and invite the children to demonstrate their ideas by moving their squirrels. Repeat the tale.

Finally, repeat the tale again, letting the children act out the role of the squirrels without using the puppets.

Support
Make your own puppet and demonstrate the actions for the children to copy.

Extension
Let the children make up their own version of the nut hunt, with their squirrels visiting different places.

Learning objective
To show awareness of space, of themselves and of others.

Group size
Ten to fifteen children.

Home links
Ask parents and carers to make a visit to a local park and go squirrel-spotting. Ask them to collect acorns, nuts and pine-cones for an autumn display.

Autumn lanterns

What you need
Large pumpkin; sharp knife (adult use); spoons; two large bowls; felt-tipped pen; night-light. For the soup: access to a microwave oven; blender; large bowl; wooden spoon; large measuring jug; kettle; onion; two vegetable stock cubes; one and a half pints of water; 45g margarine; one tablespoon each of lemon and orange juice; half teaspoon of ground ginger; salt and pepper.

Preparation
Cut off the top of the pumpkin and chop the onion.

What to do
Ask the children to wash their hands thoroughly. Encourage them to pass around the pumpkin and talk about how it feels, looks and smells. Invite them to use the spoons in turn to scoop out the orange pulp and put it carefully into the bowls, separating the flesh from the seeds.

When the pumpkin is hollowed out, ask each child to draw one feature of a face onto the outside skin. Let the children watch as you cut through the skin to make the eye, nose and mouth holes. Put the pumpkin on a secure surface in a dark corner and put a night-light in it. Talk about how the light shines through the cuts and looks like a face.

Now let the children take turns to help make the soup. First, microwave the onions and margarine in a covered bowl on high for about three minutes, until soft. When this has cooled down, add the pumpkin flesh and stir well. Stress the safety aspects of working with hot water and then make up the stock, letting the children crumble the cubes. Add this to the pumpkin mix and stir well. Add the lemon juice, orange juice, ginger and seasoning and stir again.

Cover the bowl and microwave on high for about ten minutes, or until the pumpkin is soft. Leave to cool then blend till smooth. Serve at snack time with toast or bread, with the lit pumpkin as a decoration.

Support
Invite a helper in to prepare the soup for the children to enjoy later.

Extension
Write out the recipe and encourage the children to read it with you and follow the instructions.

Learning objective
To use a range of small and large equipment.

Group size
Four or five children.

Home links
Ask parents and carers to make pumpkin lanterns with their children and send them the recipe for pumpkin soup to try themselves!

Drum procession

What you need

A collection of large plastic containers (such as ice-cream tubs); empty cylindrical containers (like coffee or custard tubs); large empty tins – with no sharp edges; polythene, rubber or fabric sheets; a selection of wools, ribbons or fabric strips in red, green and gold colours; strong sticky tape; scissors; a selection of drums and beaters.

Preparation

Make a model drum to show the children (see illustration below).

What to do

Explain that Ethiopians love celebrating New Year by beating drums. Show the children different drums and let them take turns to play them. Talk about how they are played by hand or by beaters.

Show the children your prepared drum and invite them to look at the way it is constructed – particularly the way the skin is stretched tightly and how it is fixed.

Discuss the different containers available and let the children choose one as a drum base. Invite each child select a suitable 'skin' and help them to cut it to size, stretch it over the base and fix it firmly with strong tape. Ask the children to demonstrate playing their drums with their hands and with different hard and soft beaters. Next, let them choose red, green and gold streamers to decorate their drums. When these are completed, let the children practise playing softly, loudly, slowly and rapidly, listening to one another and noticing any differences in the sounds which are made. Finally, let the children march around the room in a group, playing their drums.

Support

Help the children by pre-cutting the 'skins' to fit the bases. Use large plastic or cardboard containers which will be easier for them to manage.

Extension

Encourage the children to stretch and fix their own 'skins' once you have fastened one side for them. Challenge them to experiment and discover whether rectangular or round bases make the best drums.

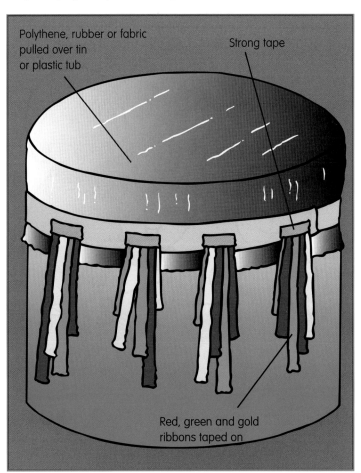

Polythene, rubber or fabric pulled over tin or plastic tub

Strong tape

Red, green and gold ribbons taped on

Learning objective
To use a range of small and large equipment.

Group size
Four or five children.

Lantern parade

What you need
Transparent, plastic pop bottles; a copy of the photocopiable sheet on page 77 for each child; felt-tipped pens or crayons; scissors; glue; coloured tissue paper; hole-punch; soft bendy wire; tape of Chinese music (if possible); string.

Preparation
Cut off the top of each bottle, leaving a base about 10cm high. Hole-punch two small holes either side of the top edge. Cut the wire into handle-sized lengths. Cut tissue paper to lengths to fit the interior of the lantern.

What to do
Tell the children that at the Moon Festival, Chinese people enjoy lantern parades. Explain to the group that they are going to make pretend lanterns (without candles) ready for a parade and talk about safety and the dangers of fire.

Give each child a photocopiable sheet and let them colour in the moon shapes brightly and cut them out. Put these safely on one side. Give each child a plastic base and let them select coloured tissue paper which they then push around the inside surface of the lantern. Help them to fix this in place by gluing the tissue over the rim of the bottle base. Invite them to stick their cut-out moon shapes in a pattern on the outside of the lantern. Talk about the different colours and designs they have chosen.

Finally, help each child to push the wire ends through the holes in the plastic and form a carrying handle.

When the lanterns are ready, play the Chinese music and encourage the children to listen to it. Then let each child carry their lantern and move in procession around the room, moving in time to the music, gently waving their lantern. Display all the lanterns by hanging them from a string close to the window to highlight the colours.

Support
Cut lengths of tissue and use them, scrunched up, to completely fill the plastic bases.

Extension
Invite the children to use a prepared template to cut out the right length of tissue to line the lantern. Let them try to glue it in themselves. Suggest that they experiment with overlapping different-coloured tissue papers.

Home links
Ask parents and carers to talk about safety and never playing with matches or naked flames.

Harvest houses

What you need
Very large cardboard box (a kitchen appliance packing case would be best); sharp craft knife (adult use); several bamboo garden canes; garden twine; thin wire; several leafy branches; scissors; apples, pears, grapes, lemons and oranges; thick brushes; yellow, white and brown thick paint; mixing pots.

Preparation
Cut two sides out of the box and cut grooves in the open top section (see illustration).

What to do
Tell the children the story of Sukkot and how many Jewish families build a special 'sukkah' in the garden to remind them of the years the Jewish people spent in the wilderness living in simple shelters.

At Sukkot, Jewish families eat some meals in the sukkah. Show the children the box and invite them to mix the paints to make different wood colours. Paint the box to look like planks of wood. Leave it to dry. Explain that the roof is open to the sky, but covered with branches and leaves for protection. Tell the children that the branches are usually decorated with hanging fruit to remember the good harvest. Talk about bamboo being a woody plant (actually the biggest member of the grass family) and show the children the canes. Use the branches to cover each cane, encouraging the children to wind garden twine around the poles to fasten them firmly. As each cane is

covered, slot it into a groove to secure it. Talk about the different fruit and show the children how to wrap wire around each piece, letting each child have a turn. As the fruit is wired, let the children take it in turns to tie the fruit to a cane to decorate the sukkah. When this is complete, let the children sit in the sukkah and share some fruit

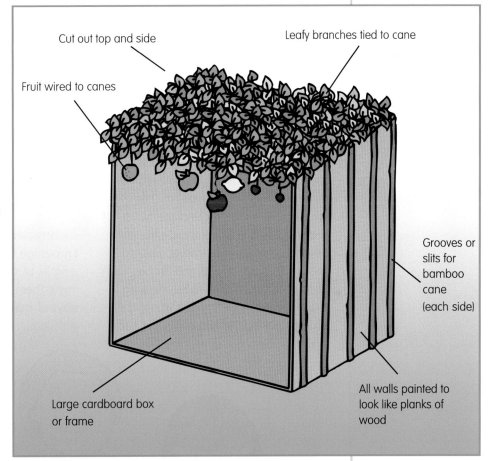

Cut out top and side

Leafy branches tied to cane

Fruit wired to canes

Grooves or slits for bamboo cane (each side)

Large cardboard box or frame

All walls painted to look like planks of wood

together. If the box is too small for the children, have a toys' sukkot meal inside.

Support
Invite the children to draw or colour in fruit shapes and hang these from hooks made from opened-up paper clips.

Extension
Let the children make their sukkah from two large boxes, joining them together with strong tape.

Learning objective
To construct safely and with increasing control.

Group size
Four to six children.

Home links
Ask parents and carers to go shopping with their children to look for unusual fruit and to find out which countries they have come from.

Learning objective
To handle tools,
objects and materials
safely and with
increasing control.

Group size
Three or four children.

Harvest dolls

What you need
Straw (or art straws or raffia); sticky tape; scissors; different-coloured wool; small silk flowers (or pictures of flowers and glue).

Preparation
Make a harvest doll to show the children. Cut the straw into appropriate lengths for the body and arm sections.

What to do
Show the children your doll and explain that harvest dolls are often made to decorate homes and tables for harvest-supper celebrations. Demonstrate to the children how to take a bundle of long straw lengths and then wrap tape around the top of this. Help each child to do the same. Next, show them how to wrap the coloured wool of their choice very tightly around the 'waist' of the straw and tie it firmly. Demonstrate how to tie another length of wool to make the 'neck' of the doll and let each child choose coloured wool, helping them to fix this firmly. Talk about the emerging shape of the body and the

'skirt' of the doll. Suggest that the children look closely at your doll and ask how they think they can make arms. Take the bundles of shorter straw lengths and show them how to wrap the ends, leaving tufts of straw to form the 'hands'. Let each child select their wool and then help them to bind the ends. Show them how to feed the arm sections through the body to complete the doll. When they have done this, let them choose silk flowers and push these into the figure to decorate it attractively. If you are using pictures, let the children cut these out and stick the flowers onto their dolls as decorations.

Support
Prepare and tie the two separate parts of the doll and let the children assemble and decorate them.

Extension
Encourage the children to cut suitable lengths of straw to make their dolls and invite them to experiment with different ways of making dolls, including dolls with legs.

Home links
Ask parents and carers to send in different types of bread, cheese and fruit and invite them to join you for a simple harvest tea.

Stick dances

What you need

Two wooden dowelling rods (about 2cm in diameter and 15cm long) for each child; brightly coloured felt-tipped pens; collection of ribbons or thick wool lengths (each about 20cm long); sticky tape; tapes of well-known nursery rhymes and songs; clear space; table.

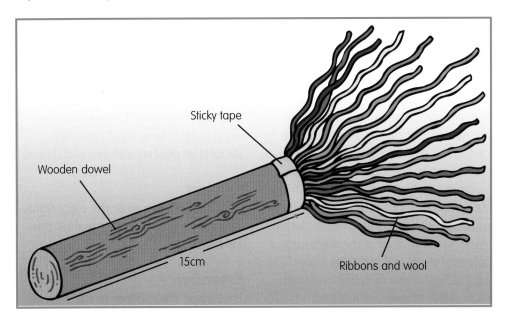

Wooden dowel

Sticky tape

15cm

Ribbons and wool

Preparation

Make a demonstration rod to show the children (see illustration above).

What to do

Tell the children that at Navaratri, Hindus remember their goddess Durga by enjoying stick dances. Show the group your prepared rod and talk about the different patterns and colours and the dangling ribbons.

Give each child two rods and let them use the felt-tipped pens to cover them with matching bright patterns. Invite them to select ribbons or wool and help them to tape these to one end of each rod, making a matching pair. Explain that these sticks can be used in dances.

Invite the children to listen to a taped song. Demonstrate how to tap out the rhythm on the table with the ends of your rods. Encourage all the

children to join in. Play the tape again and ask them to stand in a clear space. Suggest that they tap their two rods together to beat out the rhythm for the first verse and then bend down and tap both their rod ends on the floor for the second verse. For the next verse, invite them to tap their rods over their heads, slowly turning around as they do so. Repeat and let them tap out the rhythm, holding the sticks behind their backs. Next, invite the children to stand in pairs and tap out the rhythm gently against their partners' rods.

Finally, put all the different sections of the dance together and guide the children by leading the actions. Choose different music and encourage the children to find different ways of tapping their sticks safely.

Support

Ask the children to make just one rod.

Extension

Encourage the children to work in a small group and invent their own safe tapping dance. Ask them to work in pairs and also in circles, tapping everyone else's rod at least once.

Welcome lights

Learning objective
To handle tools and malleable materials safely and with increased confidence.

Group size
Six to eight children.

What you need
Clay; boards; simple clay tools; thick paints; paintbrushes; night-lights; illustrations of Divali diva lamps; long tapers and matches.

Preparation
Make two or three different divas to show the children.

What to do
Give each child a lump of clay and a board. Explain that clay is a natural substance that comes from the ground in some areas. Talk about things that are made from clay and how it needs to be fired to make a permanent change, such as for mugs and plates.

Let the children experiment with the clay and talk about how it feels and what happens when they roll it, flatten it and shape it. Now show them your prepared divas and tell them that people light these to celebrate Divali. Look at the shapes, colours and patterns of divas in the illustrations you have collected and ask each child to roll their piece of clay into a ball shape. Give them a night-light and talk about its shape and size. Ask them to use their fingers and thumbs to shape their diva so that the night-light will fit inside safely. When the shape is completed, let each child choose different clay tools to make marks and patterns on the surface. Encourage the children to look at one another's work and talk about the differences and similarities. Leave the divas to dry overnight and, the next day, invite the children to paint them.

Finally, put the divas on a safe surface and help each child to light their own lamp using a long taper. Stress the dangers of playing with fire and flames.

Support
Help the children to fit the night-lights into their divas. Light the night-lights for them.

Extension
Encourage the children to use the clay tools to make pierced holes and patterns in the clay.

Home links
Ask parents and carers to play 'I spy a lamp' and to see how many different sorts of light sources they can discover together. Ask the children to bring in examples of light sources for a display.

Whizzers and bangers

What you need
A length of ribbon for each child (about one metre long and 2cm wide); large space, indoors or outside.

What to do
Encourage the children to spread out in the space so that they are clear of one another. Tell them that these are their special spots. Ask them to look and see who is standing near them and whether they are close to a window, door or particular part of the room or area. Ask them to warm up by walking very fast around the whole space and returning to sit on their own spots. Then ask them to run, hop, jump around and return to the same spots. Can they put their hands on their chests and feel their hearts beating very fast? Explain that this is because their hearts are working hard.

Talk to the children about fireworks and the different noises, shapes and patterns they make. Ask them to pretend to be rockets, staying very low as the fuse burns and then whooshing up in the sky. Invite them to make the appropriate sound effects and follow your lead. Repeat with movements and sounds for spinning Catherine wheels, jumping crackers, Roman candles and bangers.

Now give each child a ribbon. Ask them to choose a firework and make the movements, letting the ribbons make patterns in the air as they move. Let half the group observe the others, then swap over, discussing the different patterns and shapes they see.

Ask the children to pair up and hold hands with their ribbons in their free hands. Invite each pair to make up a firework movement together to show to the rest of the group. Take turns to observe and perform, inviting the group to comment on the most exciting patterns.

Support
Let the children follow your moves, and invite helpers to assist them when working in pairs or small groups.

Extension
Encourage the children to build up a sequence of several different movements, going from one firework movement to another and making their own sound effects.

Learning objective
To move with confidence, imagination and safety.

Group size
Whole group.

Home links
Ask parents and carers to play musical fireworks – they play music for the children to dance to and, when the music is stopped, the children must move like different fireworks.

Learning objective
To recognize the
changes that happen
to their bodies when
they are active.

Group size
Whole group.

Nine candles

What you need
Large, clear space; 36 small candles; four small buckets; a hanukiah (if possible).

What to do
Tell the children about the Jewish festival of Hanukkah. Explain that at this time, Jewish people light nine candles in a special candlestick called a hanukiah to remember how the lights lasted in the temple.

Put the children into four teams and ask them to sit at one end of the space. Lay out nine candles in a row in front of each team, leaving about 20cm between each one and placing a bucket at the far end.

Ask the children to talk about how they feel. Are they hot? Cold? Can they feel their hearts beating? Take one child by the hand and help them to demonstrate how to walk to the far end, collecting one candle and placing it in the bucket, then returning for the second one and so on until all the candles have been collected. Explain that this is a slow walking game and not a race. Challenge each team and each child within it in turn to do the collecting game, counting the candles out loud as they collect them.

Ask the children how they feel now, repeating the earlier questions. Can they explain why there are any differences? Now tell them that the candle game will be a race to see which team can finish first. Ask the teams to race

and let the winners put the candles into the hanukiah if you have one. Ask the children the questions once more: are their hearts beating faster? Do they feel hot? Are they perspiring? Do they feel tired? Explain the different reactions that human bodies have when they exercise and how this is good for us – building up strong muscles (including the heart) and keeping us healthy. Repeat the races and let the children sit quietly and cool down as you tell them the story of Hanukkah and the nine candles in the hanukiah.

Support
Put the candles closer together and ask helpers to assist each child with collecting the candles.

Extension
Repeat the races, inviting the children to move in different ways – crawling, hopping and so on.

Wrap up warmly

Learning objective
To recognize the importance of keeping healthy and those things which contribute to this.

Group size
Eight to ten children.

What you need
A collection of coats, scarves, hats and gloves, sufficient for each child (these can be the children's own clothes, supplemented where necessary).

What to do
Talk with the children about the weather. What did they wear to come to the group today? Why did they wear these clothes? Discuss the importance of keeping warm and dry in cold weather in order to stay healthy. Look at different types of warm clothing together, talking about the different materials that are used. Tell the children that they are going to play a warm dressing game. Put all the hats in the centre of the space and talk about the different types, who they belong to (if appropriate) and ways in which they keep the children warm. Have a race to see who can put their hat on first. Introduce the coats and repeat the activity, helping younger children with the fastenings. Gradually add the scarves and gloves and repeat the

dressing races. Vary the game by asking for different combinations of clothes, such as scarves and gloves, or hats and scarves. Encourage the children to choose which items are to be worn. To make it more challenging, blindfold individual children in turn and let them select clothes and dress themselves appropriately, seeing how long each one takes. Finally, have a complete dressing race, and see who can dress themselves the fastest!

Support
Let the children put the coats on without fastening them up for most of the races.

Extension
To make the game more challenging, add a mixture of other winter and summer clothes, such as fleeces, sweaters, T-shirts, sandals, sun-glasses, sun-hats and wellington boots. Ask the children to respond appropriately when you say the words 'summer day' or 'winter day'.

Home links
Ask parents and carers to help their children to practise and learn how to fasten their winter coats and winter shoes. Make a chart of 'We can fasten our own coats' and complete this, sending stickers (or certificates) home to acknowledge success.

Slippery ice

What you need
Large clear space (inside or outdoors); ropes; hoops; chalk.

What to do
Talk to the children about winter weather and how frost and ice can make the roads and pavements very slippery. Stress the importance of keeping safe and not sliding on pathways because this might make others, particularly the elderly, fall and hurt themselves.

Explain to the children that they are going to play a game where they have to move in ways as if they were on slippery ice. Give each child a rope and tell them to stretch it into a straight line. Ask them to walk slowly along it, turning around and returning along its length. Now ask them to jump along and across the straight rope, turning around as before. Next, invite them to make a curly pattern with their rope, as if they were on slippery ice. Encourage them to walk carefully along these patterns and back, then to jump across and along them as before. Repeat the activity asking them to make a different curly pattern.

After a while, stop and let all the children see the varieties of slippery ice patterns that have been made. Let individual children demonstrate how they can move along their patterns. Leave the ropes in place and ask each child to move to another rope and walk and jump along that pattern. Repeat several times.

Finally, choose two or three children and ask them to chalk very long curly patterns and place a hoop at the end of each one. Put the children into teams and invite them to take turns to travel along these lines in one direction only, finishing with a big jump into the hoop when they are safely off the ice!

Support
Chalk out the long wavy patterns for the children and help them to make their rope patterns.

Extension
Let the children join up with one or more partners to make a long rope pattern course, placing hoops between the ropes and at each end to make 'safe' areas.

Traffic-lights

What you need
A large clear space; chalk or painted road markings; card and paint for a large circular sign; vehicles to ride on or toys to push around.

Preparation
Make a large circular sign, painted red on one side and green on the other, labelled 'stop' and 'go'.

What to do
Talk to the children about the vehicles they see on the roads and what makes the traffic stop and go. Stress the importance of road safety and the Green Cross Code. Explain that in winter time, when the days are darker, we need to take even more care. Discuss the dangers of heavy rain, fog, icy roads and snow and the problems drivers have in seeing people and other vehicles and stopping in time.

Ask each child to find a space on their own. Explain that when you say 'go!' they must walk around and when you say 'stop!' they must halt at once. Repeat this, encouraging them to move faster and in different ways. Then introduce the 'stop/go' sign and explain that red is for 'stop' and green is for 'go'. Talk about what would happen if vehicles did not obey the traffic-lights. Explain to the children that this time they must look carefully and watch for the change rather than hearing your voice. Hold up 'go' and, when the children have started moving, change the sign to 'stop' quickly. Repeat the activity several times, varying the time delay. Choose children to come and operate the sign and vary the movements with hopping, jumping, pigeon steps and big strides.

Finally, chalk out or use existing crossroads markings. Put the children into teams, with some acting as pedestrians wanting to cross the road and others driving vehicles or pushing toy cars. Use the traffic signs to control the traffic, letting each child operate the signs in turn.

Support
Provide adult support for the team traffic activity.

Extension
Introduce traffic-light sequence signs. Prepare a box with three traffic-light circles on each face, painted in the correct sequence, and use this to signal.

Learning objective
To move with confidence, imagination and in safety.

Group size
Whole group.

Home links
Let parents and carers know that you are working on road safety and ask them to reinforce this at home.

Wind, rain and snow

Learning objective
To move with confidence, imagination and in safety.

Group size
Eight children up to the whole group.

What you need
Clear space (inside or outside); three large sheets of card; hole-punch; felt-tipped pens; string; tape recorder and lively music such as Vivaldi's *Four Seasons – Winter*.

Preparation
Make three large card signs, drawing on symbols or pictures of windy, rainy and snowy days plus the words 'wind' 'rain' and 'snow'. Punch holes at the top of each sign and thread string through to form a hanging point.

What to do
Talk to the children about weather in winter and ask them to describe the things that they see and do in wind, rain and snow. Encourage them to find and stand in a space where they cannot touch anyone else. Talk about windy weather and suggest that they move on the spot as if they are being blown about. Ask them to move like washing blowing in the wind, a kite flying high in the sky and tree branches in a gale. Then ask them to move around the area, twisting and turning like leaves blown off trees, then being people chasing their hats or walking into a strong wind. Stop, compare movements and invite the children to demonstrate their ideas. Repeat with rainy and then snowy-weather movements such as jumping in puddles or putting up umbrellas, making snowmen or throwing snowballs, and so on.

Finally, show the children the signs and put them up on different sides of the space. Explain that they must listen to the music and when it stops you will call out 'wind', 'rain' or 'snow' and they must run to the right sign as quickly as possible. Practise a few times and then play the game, with the last one being 'out'. Vary the game by asking the children to move appropriately for the weather instruction!

Support
Keep the groups small and let helpers support the children as they run to the different signs. Congratulate the first ones there, but do not eliminate the last ones.

Extension
Introduce more weather signs, such as sun and fog, and ask the children to run in pairs, threes and fours.

Home links
Ask parents and carers to watch the television weather forecast with their children, drawing their attention to the different symbols.

Footprints

What you need
Several sheets of A4 paper for each child; pencils; scissors; Blu-Tack; clear space for safe movement.

What to do
Talk with the children about how we can often see footprints in the frost and snow and so we know where people, birds and animals have been.

Explain to the children that they are going to make paper footprints to make a trail. Demonstrate how to stand on the paper, draw round your feet and cut the footprints out. Invite each child to cut out several footprints.

Next, choose two children to lay their footprints out in two separate lines, showing them how to use Blu-Tack to fix them to the floor. Divide the group into two teams and let each team try to walk on the footprint trails. Invite two other children to add their footprints to the trails, this time in a different direction. Let the teams follow the new, longer trails. Now ask a further two children to add their footprints, adding some twists and turns to the trails. Finally, invite the other children to add their footprints to make the two trails join into one long one, with everyone walking along it.

Now collect the paper footprints and tell the children that they will play a game of *invisible* footprints. Encourage them to take turns to act as leader, walking in different directions and ways with the rest of the group following behind them and replicating their movements.

Support
Draw out a series of footprints for the children to cut out and use.

Extension
Invite the children to work in pairs to create pathways of footprints which include different ways of moving, such as jumps and slow and fast movements. Let them devise a sequence of their movements to demonstrate to others.

Learning objective
To show awareness of space, themselves and of others.

Group size
Ten to fifteen children.

Home links
Ask parents and carers to help their children look out for different types of footprints. Ask them to draw the patterns and send them in for a display or a 'Footprint detective' book.

Snowman skittles

What you need

An empty washing-up liquid bottle for each child; water or sand (to fill the bottles); jug; funnel; a copy of the photocopiable sheet on page 78 for each child; felt-tipped pens or coloured pencils; scissors; PVA glue; strong adhesive tape; beanbags; small balls.

What to do

Explain to the children that they are going to make snowmen skittles for some games.

Give each child an empty plastic bottle and help them to add a little water or sand using a jug and a funnel. Carefully wipe the top of each filled container and show the children how to seal it firmly with strong tape.

Give each child a photocopiable sheet and ask them to colour and decorate the snowman. Let them cut the snowman out carefully and glue it to the front of their bottle. If necessary, help them to fasten their snowman more securely with tape.

Set the snowmen skittles up, about two metres in front of the children and give each child a beanbag. Demonstrate how to slide a beanbag, or gently throw it to knock the skittle over. Let the children try this in turn and discuss how to be accurate by taking careful aim and controlled movement.

Invite the children to sit in pairs, about three metres apart, facing each other. Put their skittles between them and suggest that they take turns to knock the skittles down, using beanbags and then rolling a ball. Ask them to keep count of how many times they knock them over.

Finally, divide the group into two teams and place each team in a row opposite all their skittles in a matching line. Let the children take turns to roll a ball repeatedly until they knock down one skittle and all the skittles are toppled.

Support

Invite the children to throw from only one metre away and group all the skittles together.

Extension

Add numbers to the skittles and play games aiming to knock down the highest score of skittles.

Learning objective
To use a range of small and large equipment.

Group size
Six to eight children.

Home links
Ask parents and carers to use empty plastic containers to make a set of skittles. Send beanbags or balls home to enable them to play skittle games with their children.

Advent Crown game

What you need
An Advent Crown (a circular base with four candles spaced evenly around, decorated with foliage and ribbons); large space; chalk; four skittles; card; felt-tipped pens; tape recorder; music.

Preparation
Make the Advent Crown. Label four large cards with numerals 1 to 4.

What to do
Explain that Advent is the period of four weeks leading up to Christmas and that for each week a candle is lit on the Advent Crown, all four being lit for Christmas itself.

Ask the children to find a space to themselves and invite them to move around to the music. When the music stops, the children must stop, listen to you calling out a number and respond by getting into groups of this size. Play the game for a few minutes, changing the numbers swiftly so that no children are 'out' for more than a few moments. Repeat the activity, but this time hold up a numeral card for the children to read and respond to.

Next, chalk a large circle on the floor and stand skittles around to represent the candles. Invite all the children to dance around the outside. When the music stops, they must run to stand at a 'candle'. The first one to a 'candle' wins that 'candle', takes it and sits inside the circle. Repeat for the remaining three candles. Once all the candles have been won, let the winners process around the circle holding their candles, with the other children following behind. Repeat the game, letting different children be the leaders (by, for example, choosing the last one to the candle to be the winner).

Finish the session by asking all the children to stand around the circle and join in the action rhyme, counting on their fingers:

> 'Advent time, advent time, four candles to light
> One candle the first week, shining so bright
> Two candles the second week, gleam in the night
> Three candles the third week, burning so clear
> Four candles the fourth week, and Christmas is here!'

Support
Help the children by reading out the numeral cards.

Extension
Make the Advent circle as large as possible to make the game more challenging.

Learning objective
To show awareness of space, themselves and of others.

Group size
Eight to twelve children.

Home links
Ask parents and carers to buy Advent calendars and let their children open a new 'window' with them every day throughout December.

Under the tree

Learning objective
To handle tools, objects, construction and malleable materials safely and with increasing control.

Group size
Four to six children.

What you need
Christmas wrapping paper cut into different sizes; range of boxes and other similar containers; a selection of small objects for gifts; tissue paper; adhesive tape; scissors; ribbon; decorative bows and trimmings; gift tags; pencils.

What to do
Explain that people wrap Christmas presents to make them look beautiful and exciting and to keep the gift as a surprise until it is opened. Tell the children that they are going to prepare some presents for the group's teddies and toys to go under the Christmas tree.

Show the children the wrapping paper and talk about the colours, patterns and designs and the size of each sheet. Now show them the surprise gifts and let them pass them around. Talk about what size of box will be needed for each one. Choose one gift and let the children choose an appropriate box for it. Demonstrate how to select paper big enough and then wrap the box up, showing the children how to fold and cover it with wrapping paper, taping it securely. Let each child choose a gift and materials and wrap their present. Compare progress regularly and provide help as necessary. When the gifts are wrapped, let the children choose ribbons and so on to decorate them attractively.

Finally, help each child to write or copy a gift tag and put their gift under the tree.

Support
Let the children cover shoeboxes and use paper already cut to size. Alternatively, provide tin foil to use as wrapping paper as it will stay folded in place more easily.

Extension
Let the children wrap differently shaped objects without putting them inside boxes. Encourage them to make their own gift tags and write their Christmas messages and greetings on these.

Home links
If you are intending to have a Christmas party, ask parents and carers to supply gifts costing no more than £1 (or an agreed figure). Ask them to help their children to wrap them at home and bring them to school to put under the tree. Each child will take home another's gift!

Party time!

What you need
Newspaper; the photocopiable sheet on page 79; card; envelopes; sticky tape; hoops; ropes; skittles; balancing and climbing equipment; taped music.

Preparation
Enlarge the photocopiable sheet to A3 size and mount it onto card, cut out the individual cards and put them into envelopes. Make a 'Pass the parcel' package from wrapped layers of newspaper with envelopes placed between each layer. Set out the skittles, hoops, ropes and larger equipment.

What to do
Explain that Muslims celebrate the festival of Eid at the end of Ramadan (the month when they fast during daylight hours). Celebrations include visiting friends and family and enjoying parties. Children celebrating at school sometimes play games like 'Pass the parcel'.

Explain to the children that they are going to play a game like 'Pass the parcel' but with special actions. Invite them to sit in a circle near the equipment and show them how to pass the parcel around, playing the taped music and turning it off from time to time. Explain that when the music stops, they must stop passing the parcel around. Let them practise this a few times and then tell them that this time the child who is holding the parcel when the music stops may take one layer off. Play the tape and then stop it.

Help the child to unwrap one layer and find the envelope. Ask them to take out the card and show it to all the children. Look at the picture and read the instruction together. Then encourage the 'winner' to perform the action. Ask the rest of the group 'Did he (or she) do it correctly?', reminding them of the direction under, over and so on. Invite volunteers to demonstrate another way of doing the same action, again stressing the need for accuracy. Continue playing the game until all the children have had several turns.

Support
Limit the range of cards and equipment and help the children with their actions where necessary.

Extension
Make more complex instruction cards linking more than one action such as 'Jump over the skittles and climb through the climbing frame'.

Learning objective
To travel around, under, over and through balancing and climbing equipment.

Group size
Eight to ten children.

Home links
Ask parents and carers to make their own 'Pass the parcel' games. Send home a sheet of instruction labels with simple activities such as 'Sit on the floor', 'Go up the stairs' or 'Open the door' for them to use.

Learning objective
To move with confidence, imagination and in safety.

Group size
Eight to ten children.

Backwards and forwards

What you need
Large space; one hoop, rope and beanbag for each child.

What to do
Talk about New Year and how people often think back over the past year and look forward to the new one.

Tell the children that they are going to play some backwards and forwards games. Invite them to stand in a line facing you. Ask them to step forwards and stop, then step backwards and stop. Ensure they do not turn around to move! Repeat the activity jumping, running, rolling and hopping.

Next, give out the ropes and ask the children to stretch them out in a straight line. Let the children jump forwards and then move backwards across the ropes. Repeat the task, inviting the children to demonstrate to one another.

Now give out the hoops, one for each child. Ask them to step forwards into the hoop and backwards out of it. Select children to demonstrate their movements and ask them to choose different ways of moving backwards and forwards in and out of the hoops. Talk about their different methods and let the other children copy some of them.

Arrange the hoops around the space and give out a beanbag to each child. Ask them to move around the space and, when they reach a hoop, place their beanbag inside it. Then tell them to move on to a filled hoop and pick the beanbag up, moving forwards to fill another empty hoop – only one bag per hoop. Encourage the children to vary the movements between hoops – hopping, crawling and so on.

Finally, repeat the activity but ask the children to move backwards between the hoops.

Support
Place the ropes and hoops yourself and let the children take turns to move forwards and backwards. Invite helpers to hold their hands when necessary.

Extension
Lay out the ropes and hoops as a circular obstacle course and encourage the children to move in different ways all around the space.

Home links
Invite parents and carers to play simple backwards and forwards games with their children, and send home a sheet with ideas for them to try.

Special gifts

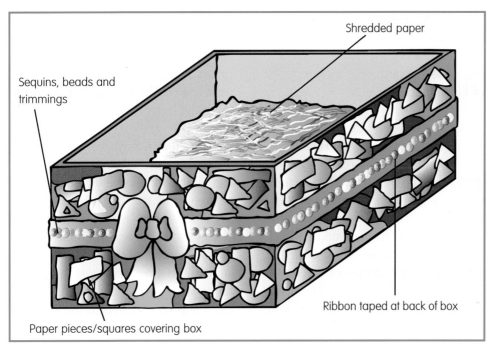

Sequins, beads and trimmings

Shredded paper

Ribbon taped at back of box

Paper pieces/squares covering box

Learning objective
To handle tools, objects and malleable materials safely and with increasing control.

Group size
Four children.

What you need
A range of cardboard boxes and containers; brightly coloured paper; scissors; glue; beads; sequins and trimmings; tying coloured ribbon; sticky tape; play dough or similar; modelling boards.

Preparation
Make a gift box tied up with a ribbon for demonstration purposes (see illustration above).

What to do
Explain to the children how in Spain, at Epiphany, children receive their Christmas gifts. Talk about the excitement of giving and receiving presents and tell the children that they are each going to make a pretty gift box and then put a surprise inside.

Look at the boxes together and let each child choose one. Discuss the range of papers that can be used to cover it. Encourage each child to cut small pieces of paper to glue onto the cardboard to cover their box. Then invite them to select trimmings to decorate the outside to make it attractive.

Ask each child to choose their favourite ribbon and help them to measure and cut a length long enough to wrap around the outside of the box and also to make a bow at the front. Invite them to use sticky tape to fasten the ribbon at the rear of the gift box, pulling the lengths to the front, and to make a bow. Provide as much assistance as is needed with this difficult task.

Finally, give out the boards and play dough and ask each child to model a surprise item to go inside their box. Talk about the different ideas they have and let them discuss their models as they progress. Suggest that they cut bright paper into shreds to line their box and then place their surprise inside.

Support
Pre-cut the covering paper into small squares to cover the box and make shredded paper to line it.

Extension
Invite the children to use card to construct closing lids for their boxes and encourage each child to add a gift tag with a written greeting.

Home links
Ask parents and carers to look at as many different gift boxes and containers as they can with their children. Suggest that they talk about how they are made and what goes in them. Ask them to send in some gift boxes to be displayed alongside the ones that the children have made.

Sunshine chasing

What you need
Large space; yellow band or strip of yellow fabric about 40cm long; large disc of yellow card; yellow chalk; tape of Indian music.

What to do
Tell the children that many Hindus celebrate the sunshine returning after the winter and that they often wear bright yellow clothes as a sign of this.

Show the children the yellow fabric and explain that they are going to play some sunshine games. Chalk a large circle 'sun' in the middle of the space and encourage the children to move around the outside. Play the tape and, when the music stops, ask the children to run into the sunshine circle as quickly as they can. Repeat several times. Vary the game by inviting the children to dance in the sun circle, dashing out and sitting down in a space when the music stops. Make the activity more difficult by chalking a smaller and smaller circle each time.

Next give each child a strip of yellow fabric and show them how to tuck one end into the back of their shorts (or equivalent), so that most of the length dangles down. Put the card sun in one corner. Ask one child to be the 'sunshine chaser' and explain that they will chase around and collect as many 'rays of sunshine' (pieces of yellow fabric) as they can while the music is playing. Invite the 'rays' to dance around the space for a few moments before you let the 'chaser' go. The 'chaser' puts each ray on the card sun as they are collected. When the music stops, everyone must stand still. Remind the group that only the chaser can touch the 'rays' and no one must touch anyone else. Repeat the activity a few times, letting each child be the 'chaser' in turn.

Support
Let the children hold the sunshine 'rays' in their hands but ask them to give them up when they are pulled.

Extension
Invite the children to have two 'chasers' at a time.

Hoop dance

Red and gold ribbons tied onto hoop

Red and yellow crêpe-paper wraps

Learning objective
To move with control and co-ordination.

Group size
Four to six children.

What you need
Large space; small hoop for each child; long strips of red and yellow crêpe paper; red and gold ribbon; tape of Chinese-style music.

What to do
Explain that at Chinese New Year, people perform a Lion Dance. Someone wears a fierce lion's head at the front and others hold up a long hoop under some fabric to form the lion's body.

Tell the children that they are going to make decorated hoops using the red and gold colours that the Chinese use for good luck (see illustration above). Explain that they will also be making up their own hoop dances.

Give each child a hoop and help them to wrap crêpe-paper strips around it, fastening each completed strip with sticky tape. Assist them with cutting the red and gold ribbons into 20cm strips, tying them securely into a bunch at the top of the hoop. Now ask the children to find a safe space in a circle with their completed hoops. Suggest that each child hold out their hoop in front of them with the ribbons furthest away, then out to each side, then above their heads. Talk about how the pattern looks as everyone does the same thing. Now play a little of the Chinese-style music and ask the children to hold the hoops in different ways, moving them to the music, but staying on the same spot. Stop and let the children look at one another's movements and invite them to copy the most interesting ones. Repeat the activity, but let the children move around in a circle, reminding them to dance without touching one another. Encourage them to practise and improve their dance, starting with the static movements and then on to the moving section when you give a signal. Perform the dance for the rest of the group. After the dance, hang the hoops up for a display.

Support
Have the hoops almost wrapped and help the children to finish them off.

Extension
Let the children work in pairs to make up a simple dance of their own, moving together and then apart.

Home links
Ask parents and carers to play simple circle dance games with their children such as 'Ring-o-Ring-o-Roses' and 'The farmer's in his dell'.

Carnival antics

What you need
A copy of the photocopiable sheet on page 80 for each child; elastic; scissors; PVA adhesive; felt-tipped pens; sequins; beads; buttons and trimmings; sticky tape; tin foil; hole-punch; card; tape of suitable parading music (such as *Carnaval de Paris* by Dario G).

Preparation
Mount the photocopiable sheets onto card and cut out the eye sections. Make a mask (see illustration below) and show the children.

What to do
Explain that at Mardi Gras, people around the world often celebrate by holding Carnival parades where they wear elaborate masks and costumes.

Give each child a photocopiable sheet and ask them to colour the mask as brightly as they can. Let them cut it out and stick on their choice of beads, buttons and sequins to make the mask really colourful and striking. Invite them to cut strips of tin foil about 20cm x 4cm. Tape these to the top of the mask so that they will dangle over the wearer's hair. Help the children to punch holes at the sides and then thread elastic through, taping the ends securely, so that the masks fit.

When the masks are dry, play the music and talk about the happy mood of the piece and why this is appropriate for celebration and parade music. Encourage the children to move

around to the music, stopping the tape frequently to let them look at one another's ideas.

Now ask the children to stand in a line and follow your movements as you lead the parade. Vary your movements – with twists, turns and jumps, and remind the children to be careful not to touch anyone else. Choose different children to act as leader.

Finally, let everyone put on their masks and practise parading to the music. Demonstrate the Carnival parade to the rest of the group, or to parents and carers.

Support
Cut out the mask shape for the children and pre-punch the holes. Prepare the foil strips yourself.

Extension
Encourage the children to design and make matching wrist decorations – for example, card cuffs fastened with elastic, decorated with sequins and dangling foil.

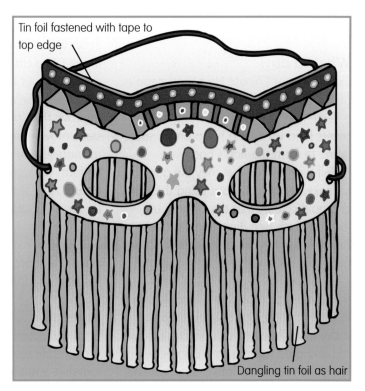

Tin foil fastened with tape to top edge

Dangling tin foil as hair

A bunch of flowers

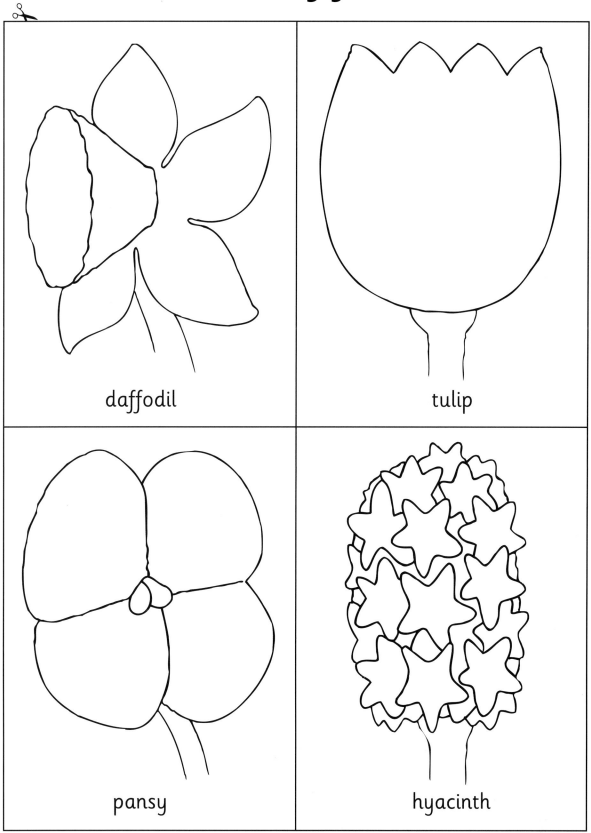

daffodil

tulip

pansy

hyacinth

Here we grow!

When we are little we lie on our backs,
lie on our backs, lie on our backs
And when we are hungry we cry for some snacks,
cry for some snacks, cry for some snacks.

Then we stretch out with our toes in the air,
toes in the air, toes in the air
We follow our mums and we crawl everywhere,
crawl everywhere, crawl everywhere.

Suddenly we're able to stand up so tall,
stand up so tall, stand up so tall
Build up brick towers and play with a ball,
play with a ball, play with a ball.

We learn to turn pages, to paint and to draw,
to paint and to draw, to paint and to draw
We climb up high stairs and can sit on the floor,
sit on the floor, sit on the floor.

Now we are older we run fast and jump high,
run fast and jump high, run fast and jump high
But if we fall over – ouch! We still give a cry,
still give a cry, still give a cry!

Pauline Kenyon

Don't disturb the tadpoles!

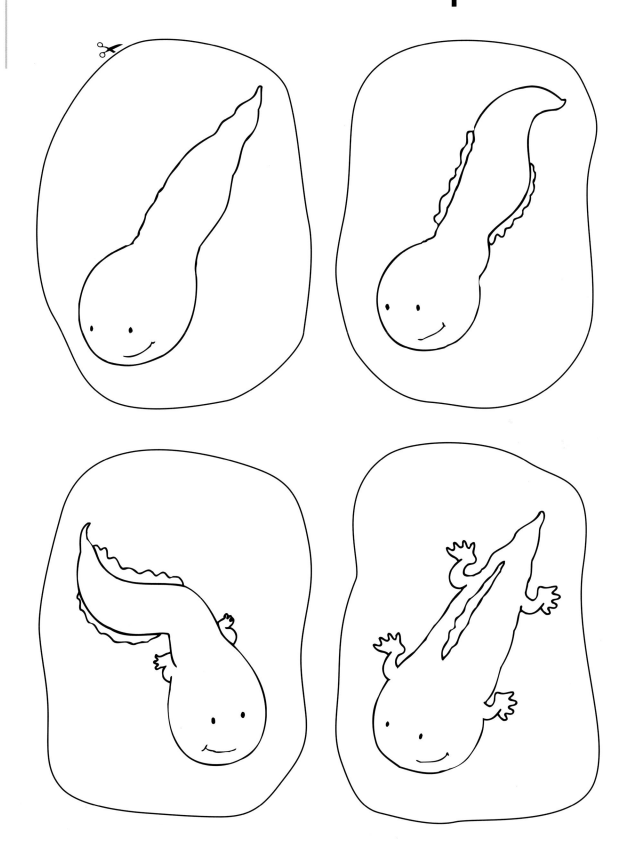

Rabbit chase

Fold back and glue

SPRING
PHOTOCOPIABLE

Baisakhi

New flags

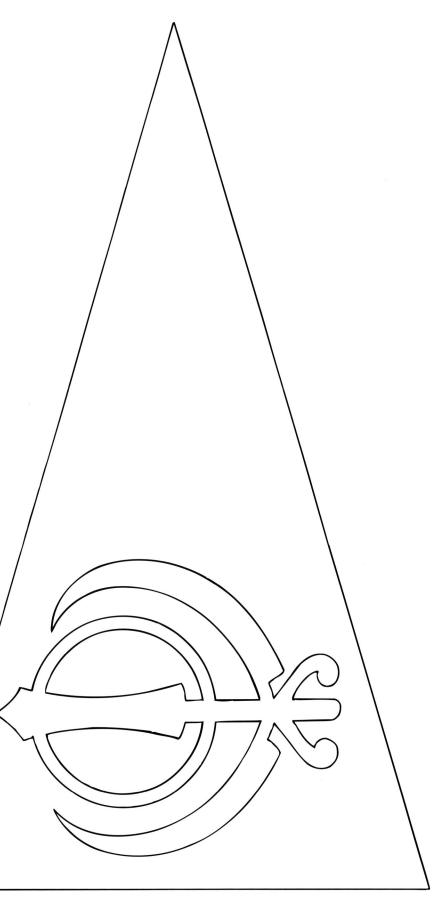

EARLY YEARS AROUND THE YEAR Physical development

69

St George and the dragon

Fish in a flap!

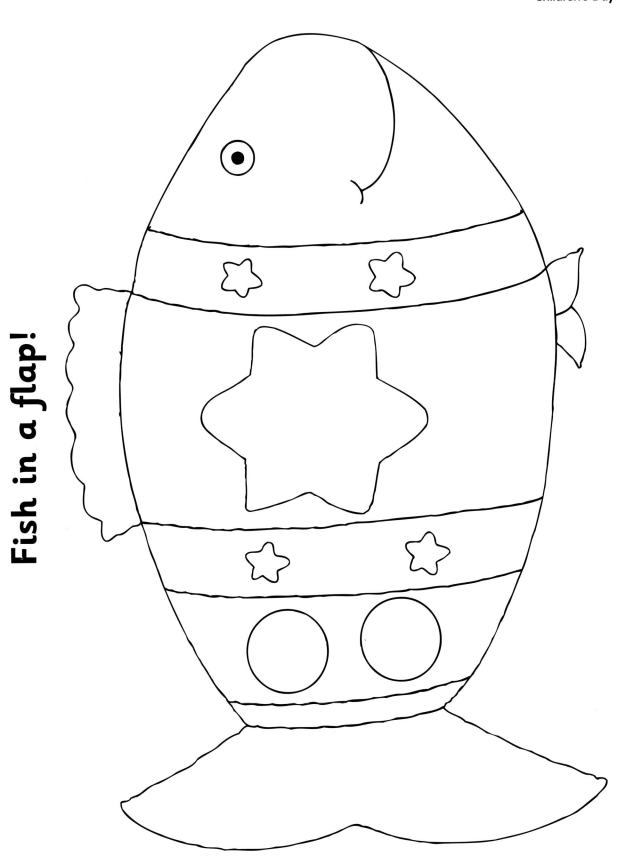

Where are the minibeasts?

Tree delights

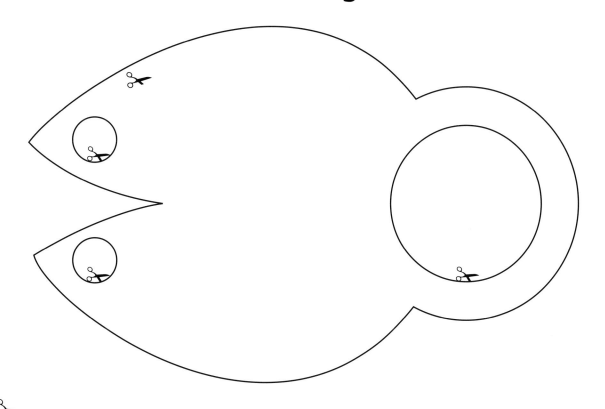

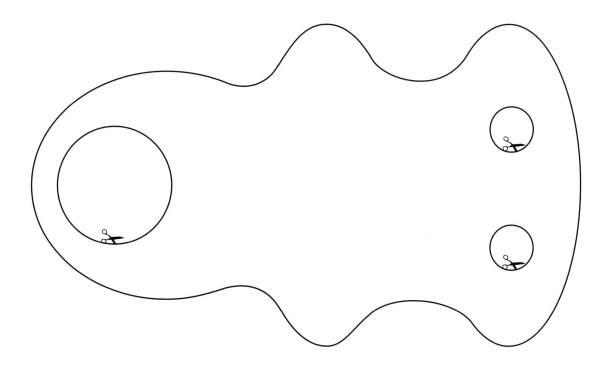

Flaming messages

EARLY YEARS AROUND THE YEAR Physical development

Floral designs

Squirrel hunt

Lantern parade

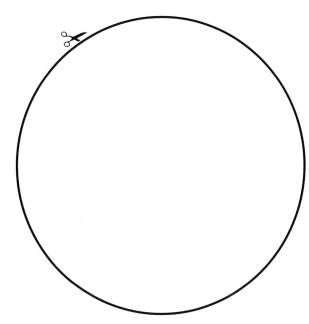

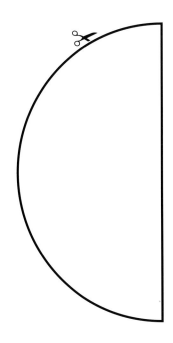

Snowman skittles

Party time!

Run around the skittles.	Go through the hoop.
Sit in the hoop.	Jump over the skittle.
Walk around the hoop.	Jump in the hoop.
Go under the frame.	Climb over the bench.
Climb on the frame.	Stand on the bench.

Carnival antics

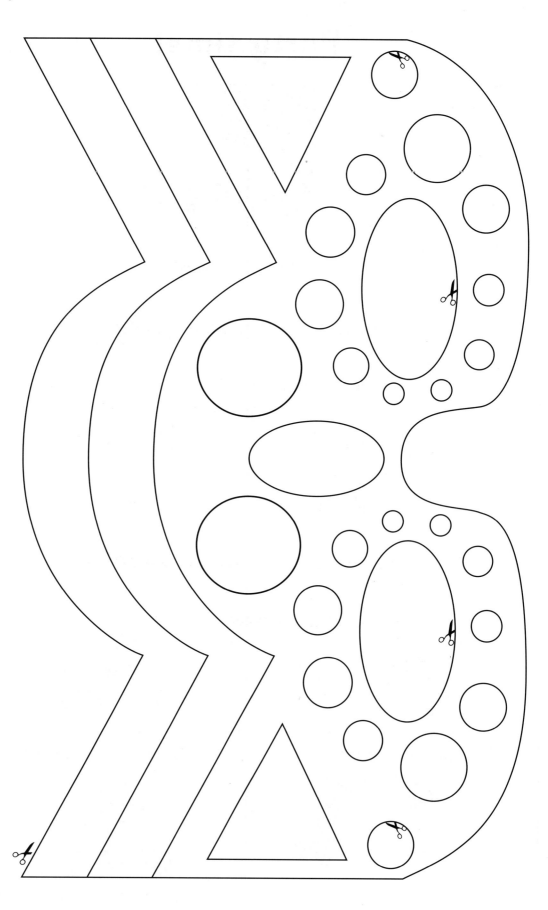

EARLY YEARS AROUND THE YEAR Physical development